HOLD ON TO
hope

CW00552350

Love Love Cassie ♡

HOLD ON TO hope

A COLLABORATIVE PROJECT BY CASSIE SWIFT

TRUE YOU
CHILDREN'S LIFE COACHING

First Published by True You Children's Life Coaching 2022
Copyright © Cassie Swift 2022

Cassie Swift has asserted her right to be identified as the author of this
Work in accordance with the Copyright, Designs and Patents Act 1988.

ISBN: 978-1-7396179-1-2

For permissions contact:
cassie@trueyouchildrenslifecoaching.co.uk

Editing and typeset by Fuzzy Flamingo
www.fuzzyflamingo.co.uk

Cover design by Heather Hulbert Designs
www.heatherhulbert.co.uk

A catalogue for this book is available from the British Library.

This book is dedicated to all the beautiful souls who have been through struggles and adversity, to let them know never, ever to give up hope! There is always that glimmer of light at the end of the tunnel, holding onto hope is what will get you through! You will find inner strength and you will come out the other side, and one day you will be able to share your story to pass that glimmer of hope onto others. Always Hold on to Hope.

Cassie Swift

DISCLAIMER:

Please be aware that this book contains topics of a sensitive nature, some of which people may find upsetting or triggering.

For permissions contact:
cassie@trueyouchildrenslifecoaching.co.uk

This book is not intended to be a comprehensive medical guide. The opinions and information expressed in this publication are those of the authors only and they are sharing their expertise, but do not represent professional advice. This book is not intended as a substitute for seeking professional medical advice and the reader should regularly consult a medical expert in matters relating to their health, particularly with respect to any symptoms that might require a diagnosis or medical attention. The authors take no responsibility for any actions taken as a result of reading this book and do not assume and hereby disclaim any liability for any losses occurring as a result.

Trigger warning: please be advised that this book talks about issues that may be triggering, including eating disorders, self-harm, suicide attempts, abuse and alcoholism.

CONTENTS

HOPE IS

Carol Barwick

"I wait for the Lord, my whole being waits, and in his word I put my hope."
– Psalms 130:5 NIV

Hope Springs
Hope Sings
Hope dreams, believes say yes.
Hope waits, excited, patient, impatient it tugs to see
what's round the corner yet spends time on its knees in
silence.
Hope grows
Under the ground, unseen it pushes its roots deep into
the earth before the fruit is seen.
Hope has been, is and will be.
Hope is critical, crucial, loudly silent and violently
peaceful.
Hope is strength when the weapons no longer have
power.
Hope is.

★★★

Dedicated to my amazing family and friends who have supported me on my long Covid journey through faith and hope.

Carol Barwick is a singer and creative writer who created and manages Raise: raising confidence, inspiring creativity.

Carol has over twenty years' experience working with a variety of different people in various settings, including being a former primary school teacher and running a community choir.

She has a 2:1 BA Hons in creative writing and music and a diploma in creative practice in community settings.

Her passion is to raise the self-esteem and confidence of everyone she works with and she firmly believes that everyone matters.

https://linktr.ee/carolbarwick

Listen to the audio version here:
https://bit.ly/HopeIsPoem

FINALLY FINDING FREEDOM AT FORTY

Cassie Swift

"Always remember you are braver than you believe, stronger than you seem, smarter than you think, loved more than you know and twice as beautiful than you ever imagined!"
– Adapted from AA Milne

Trigger warning: this chapter contains talk of eating disorders, self-harm and suicide attempts

At what point in my life do I start this chapter? Do I decide to start writing about the issues with food that I had from when I was a toddler or when it got seriously bad as a teen? I will give a quick rundown of it all to give context.

As a toddler, I was a picky eater, I wouldn't sit and eat meals and the food I ate wasn't very varied at all (nowadays it would be looked at as ARFID; Avoidant Restrictive Food Intake Disorder). It was suggested that my mum leave bowls of snacks around for me to eat, as 'I would eat when I was hungry.'

As people said, 'I then discovered food and didn't stop.'

(This too has a diagnosis now as Binge Eating Disorder.) By the time I started school, I was overweight, resulting in me being bullied the whole of my school life.

When I was around seven or eight, I had to go to a hospital dietitian to be weighed regularly and to review my diet and food and drink intake. So, as you can already see, food has always been an issue.

My mum would constantly ask if she looked fat, and she'd always be on different diets, worrying about her size. I quickly learned that weight was a serious thing and, as I already said, got bullied throughout my whole school life for it.

Starting secondary school was the worst. I was hoping it would be different, but it wasn't, and soon the bullies carried on and it was the worst it had ever been. I had no friends, and it was horrendous. At the age of around fourteen, I started going to a weekly slimming club. Why they take children this young, I do not know, but they did! I lost over three stone, received 'Slimmer of the Year' and, during this time, I also gained friends. My connection with being accepted and losing weight was anchored in. I was at a normal weight but still saw myself as fat and that is when the problem started, although I didn't see it until much later.

As our school prom approached, I lost a bit of weight I had gained to fit into the beautiful dress that I really, really wanted. I then lost 'too much' weight and it had to be altered a few times, but I was still okay and at a normal weight. However, unhealthy behaviours around food and disordered eating had already begun.

My parents were separated. My dad left when I was eleven, and I saw him occasionally up to the age of fourteen, but didn't see him after that until adulthood (that's a whole other story). So, we were a single parent family, something which was uncommon back then. My mum did what she thought was best for me all the time, but she was overprotective. I wasn't allowed to go out and socialise, or go to sleepovers, I wasn't even allowed to learn to ride a bike in case I hurt myself. I know she did everything out of love but unfortunately it left me with no control over anything I did.

I was a perfectionist and I put a lot of pressure on myself academically to achieve highly and do well in everything that I started. I successfully passed my GCSEs and A levels, and I got a place at university. I was the first person in the family to go to an actual university, so the pressure was still on!

I was going to read psychology – the irony is laughable. Although the university was London-based, I was going to be staying in halls of residence. It was the first time I had ever been away from home, let alone living on my own on a day-to-day basis, so it was very exciting. The weird feeling of being able to make my own decisions. I guess, looking back, it was a little overwhelming, not really knowing what I should or shouldn't do and what I could and couldn't do, because I hadn't learned any of that stuff growing up. I'd just gone from being protected and not really having freedom to living in the middle of London with a bunch of girls I'd never met before, so uni life started great.

Not having to answer to people, doing what I wanted to do, socialising, clubbing, all the things that students do. Very quickly, I became aware of how pretty the other girls were, how amazing they looked in their clothes going out and how, if I wanted people to like me at uni, I needed to lose weight. And so it began without me even realising.

I went on a diet. Looking back, I don't even know if I really needed to, but I started it and very, very quickly the diet escalated and my weight dropped. I quickly began losing weight and the foods that I ate became more and more reduced. When I would go home at weekends, my mum and my friends would comment about the weight that I had lost and I would reassure them that everything was fine because, at the time, I honestly didn't think there was anything wrong. I didn't think that only eating two slices of toast a day was not normal. I didn't see the weight falling off me. I didn't think that exercising for hours and hours at a time was a problem. It was normal. It was my new uni life that I was in control of.

Or so I thought. Soon the control flipped, and food held the control. The food restriction became more, the exercise became more, the consumption of alcohol became more, and my weight became less. I completed the first year of university with a 2:1 and had good predictions for my second year. It wasn't until that summer that things became difficult.

I had to go back home and make excuses for not eating, avoiding meals, lying, moving food around, hiding food. It was all normal and slowly I felt like the control was being taken away from me again.

The summer came and went, and I was now very slim in the second year. I moved into a flat with two other girls in the middle of London. This was to be short-lived.

Food restriction came to a point where I basically wasn't eating anything. I would drink a bit of alcohol and that was it. The numbers on the scales were going down: nine stone, eight stone, seven stone, six stone. I realised there was a problem. I lost everything; this wasn't my decision, it was made for me. I went home to see my mum and never went back to my London flat share with the view of the London Eye from my bedroom; my belongings were collected, an enormous invasion of my privacy, but I was in hospital so had no control. I lost my uni place, my new friends, my job at Wimbledon Tennis, but most of all I lost my independence and I lost myself!

It was decided it would be better for me to leave uni and move back in with my mum. This was the best and only decision, however at the time it did not feel like it; I had failed again. I was five and a half stone and, after my mum had several arguments with GPs, I was rushed to hospital. My blood was so thick that they didn't know how it was pumping around my body or how much longer it could. My body was eating my heart, as this was the only muscle left. There was literally nothing left, and they didn't know what the outcome was going to be.

I don't know how long I was in the hospital; a few weeks, I think. All I know is I had to drink loads and loads of water and I had to start eating. I sat eating lettuce and cucumber, crying because I was convinced it was going to make me fat. How on earth had things got to this point? I was twenty years old!

I remember one day on the ward round having some student doctors come round with the other consultants. I think they thought that the curtains in the hospital were soundproof because, after they'd come in to speak to me and had left, they stood outside, and I remember hearing them say, "We haven't had anyone on this ward that's ever been like this. This is the worst case we've seen; she's so thin. There's nothing of her. How is she still alive?" I remember that.

I also remember the threats of what would happen if I refused to eat anything. I was given thick, sweet drinks to drink. I refused and I was given a clear ultimatum. Control was taken away again. And my weight went up not by consuming food but by liquid, drinking high calorie drinks. I was still very underweight but was 'medically stable', so I left the hospital in a wheelchair feeling vulnerable. I had developed agoraphobia. I didn't want to go out, didn't want to see people, didn't want to speak to people. I wanted to disappear.

My whole life had been turned upside down. I'd lost my place at uni, lost my job and lost my freedom. Everything had been taken away from me and an unknown future was lying ahead of me. I would have to be an inpatient in a specialist unit and to be an inpatient you have to have a BMI of thirteen. How ridiculous is that? A healthy BMI is eighteen to twenty-five, but you're only considered 'anorexic enough' to get treatment if your BMI is below thirteen. Crazy.

Anyway, February 2003, I was admitted to an eating disorder unit. One of the best in the country. I obviously wasn't listened to. I was too ill to be listened to and didn't know what I was saying. I wasn't capable of making sense or making choices. There were two programmes in the inpatient unit. One was a restrictive anorexic programme. The other I can't remember the name of (possibly multi-impulsive) but it was one that included different behaviours such as purging, exercise, impulsiveness and I told them that was the one that I needed to be on. But they treated me as just very restrictive. Years later, they admitted that they had got it wrong. They admitted it probably did me more harm than good. It was too late by then; nothing could be undone.

So, I was now in an institution with probably about fifteen other patients, all of us 'restrictive anorexics'. The biggest part of the recovery programme was eating a 3000-calorie diet. Yep, 3000 calories, eating six times a day, which was basically all day, and once we'd reached a healthy weight, we could be discharged. Anyone on a 3000-calorie diet is going to put weight on quite quickly.

We would eat oversized portions of food and what happened was many behaviours and tricks would be shared around the ward to make it seem like we had put weight on but maybe hadn't. (I won't disclose them here, as it's not something that I am proud of and it's not something that I want others to know. But this is what happens in this style of hospital. You come out a lot worse than you went in.)

In there, all control was taken away. We were being fattened up. I wouldn't leave the unit because of the agoraphobia; although by then I had put on weight and was able to walk, the fear of the outside was too much. My depression got worse. My meds were up. My mood was so bad. And I wasn't sticking to the programme. This is when you normally got a 'timeout' when you were naughty and didn't abide by the rules that were given. You left the hospital for a week to think about your behaviour. However, they were concerned about my safety if I left, so I had 'time in', which meant I wasn't allowed out of my room. I wasn't allowed to go to art therapy or into other people's rooms. They weren't allowed to come in to see me. I even had to be accompanied in the shower, it was horrendous. I took up smoking, having not smoked until this point.

Anyway, I carried on putting on weight to reach my healthy weight and then things got really bad. I self-harmed. I'd picked this behaviour up as I had absolutely no control over what was happening to me or my body, and psychologically nothing was being done. This time I did get a timeout and, during my timeout week, I went on holiday. When I went back, I decided enough was enough and I discharged myself.

The family therapy had caused so much pain between me and my mum that when I was discharged, I couldn't go back and live with her. This obviously led to more problems. Sofa surfing became my life – neighbours, friends. Not having anywhere of my own, a friend from the unit said that I could live with her and her parents. So, I had some stability. However, after a while, I decided I needed to find somewhere else. I was technically homeless.

I'd been told by this point that I couldn't have children because of what I had done to my body. My heart was broken. All I'd ever wanted was to be a mummy and even that had now been taken away.

I came out with disordered eating that had been made worse and my self-harming behaviours increased in a variety of ways. Again, I'm not going into them, as I am not proud of them and I don't want to give people ideas. Self-harming became a way of coping, a way to control my feelings when everything else had been taken away. It was the only way to express my emotions and self-hatred.

Things became worse and late in 2003 was my first suicide attempt. I was taken to hospital where I spent New Year. I was treated like rubbish, as is often the case with suicide attempts and self-harm injuries because you are 'attention seeking' or 'wasting resources' and 'they are busy enough without wasting time on people who don't want to be here' and 'there are people here fighting for their lives who we should be seeing to'.

Then, once physically stable, came my first day in a psychiatric unit. As I write this, the memories are as clear as yesterday – something I hadn't thought about for so long but still so clear. It is the scariest place I've ever been. It was a mixed ward of gender, age and illness. The things I witnessed, the things I heard and the things I saw I wouldn't wish on my worst enemy. I actually feared for my life as one of the other patients thought I had been sent as a spy and wanted to kill me; I would be threatened and told not to sleep. (I have never spoken about any of this before and as I sit here typing I can't actually believe that this place existed and scarily still does.) I think the first stay was short (yes there was more than one stay), but I can't really remember. I do know that I was out of the hospital either on a weekend stay or had been fully discharged when I attempted it again, straight away, and went back to the unit, this time for longer. More horrific things were witnessed; I wish I could erase them from my memory, but I cannot. They are still there. I was watched continuously to check for my safety. It was just all horrific and awful.

Having studied psychology and – against the perception of mentally ill people being stupid – I was able to use the right type of language and reasoning (not that I'm proud of it) to enable me to get overnight leave. I succeeded; I had got the overnight leave I so desperately wanted with the intention of doing it again and being successful.

So, now in mid-2004, I attempted for the third time. Apparently, this was the worst one. The hospital told me how 'lucky' I was and that had I been just ten minutes later, they wouldn't have been able to save me. (Writing that feels hard to comprehend and now I am incredibly grateful to the hospital and staff, but then I was anything but.) I don't really know what happened. I remember being wired up to machines in the ICU, my mum coming in and just being awful to her and telling her to go, something I deeply regret! There were issues with my heart and organs and ability to breathe, but I honestly can't remember how long I was in there. It wasn't something that was ever really spoken about again with my mum or my family.

Needless to say, once back in the psych unit, my every move was watched. I was constantly threatened with being sedated and they were, of course, very careful before discharging me. I was in there a very long time.

Eventually, I was discharged to a friend's house, who my mum knew and who the hospital knew and had checked everything out, so you see I still wasn't in control as I 'didn't know what was best for me'. However, it was out of the hellhole, at least. I stayed there for a while and then on to someone else's sofa. Eventually, due to overcrowding, I got my own place; a time when there should be excitement and anticipation. However, everyone was worried and so I was closely monitored what felt like all the time by everyone. But I had my own front door, which I could close at the end of the day. Things were starting to look up: my own place, my own space, my first ever fur baby – my beautiful Misty who passed away in November 2019 – who was my best friend and knew my behaviour and mannerisms down to a tee.

I now had somewhere that I was safe and could call my home! I even met someone who lived in a different part of the country and a relationship started. Hope saw me through, it was all that I had. I had been to rock bottom, I had to have hope, I had been given another chance. I even got a tattoo on my ankle at the age of twenty-two – the Chinese symbol for hope because, without it, I would have had nothing. Things weren't how I'd planned them. Thinking about it now feels so surreal.

I really did think things were going to change when I met Dave; a new start to my life, my soulmate. Unfortunately, tragedy hit, but that's for another time.

But what I went through, how I felt, what I witnessed and how I was treated, looking back now, all of that formed who I am today. And clearly the hospitals were very wrong about my fertility because I have three beautiful miracle children who are my life and reason for being here.

So, if you are travelling this journey, NEVER give up hope. Always hold on to that glimmer of light. You never ever know what the future holds and what it is you are to carry out in your lifetime. But hope is something that will help you to grow. One day you will be telling your own story and being that glimmer of light in someone else's journey! I now at last share and release this part of my story that has always been there, the feelings of shame and guilt following me, and now, two decades on and as I enter the fortieth year on this planet, I can release this, I can step into being me without the worry of being found out. I found an inner strength I never knew I had, and you can too. Whatever you do, *Hold on to Hope*!

★★★

To my three beautiful, incredible daughters who are my miracles and who have taught me so much. I am grateful beyond words to be your mummy and I hope that you know how proud I am of you! You are my world, girls, and I love you more than I can put into any words!

Cassie has been described by her children as 'awesome, kind, incredible, caring, beautiful and AMAZEBALLS'. Her friends describe her as a kind-hearted, loving and courageous woman and single mother of three. She will stand up for her beliefs and the rights of others. Cassie experienced bullying throughout her entire school life, and wishes that there had been someone available to have turned to, because as a result, her mental health deteriorated. This is not something anyone would wish for a child, and no one deserves to feel this way or experience what she went through.

Cassie works as a Family Empowerment Guide, specifically with teens, to enable them to feel empowered about life. She helps them to manage big emotions in a positive way, accepting the true version of themselves. As a result, she brings calm and happiness, not only to those she works with, but to the whole family. She is trained in several holistic approaches, including NLP, EFT, hypnotherapy and EFT specifically for teens, as well as a lot of life experience, which helps to put her unique spin on things.

Cassie is also a number one best-selling author of four books, is the founder and organiser of the Children's Mental Health Matters Summit, and has appeared on the radio and in six local newspapers speaking about issues surrounding children's mental health.

"Helping others, especially children, is my passion. I want to empower as many children as I possibly can!"

https://linktr.ee/CassieS

Listen to the audio version here:
https://bit.ly/FinallyFindingFreedomatForty

BEHIND CLOSED DOORS

Ashleigh Quick

*"I now see how owning our story and loving ourselves
through that process is the bravest thing that we will ever
do. You are not the darkness you endured. You are the
light that refused to surrender."*
– Ashleigh Quick and John Green

Do you remember as a child dreaming of the princess wedding, the big white dress, the train flowing behind you down the aisle and, most importantly, the happy ever after? For me it was the horse and carriage, my father walking me down the aisle, walking bare foot on the white sandy beaches, feeling the gentle breeze through my hair, holding hands with the man I loved.

If only my childhood dreams had become my reality. Instead, I remember getting ready at home and my best and oldest childhood friend arriving to drive me to the hotel to marry a man I had known since birth, a man I wanted to trust and love till my last breath. We were running late, and all I wanted to do was say, "Jason, I don't want to marry this man," but I didn't.

I knew he wasn't perfect; perfection is a myth. We

learn, we grow and evolve, that was my hope. I believed he would change; I could change him. I believed that when I became his wife, he would love me. I could not have been more wrong. This man was my second cousin, part of my family and my father's half-sister's son. It was not until a few years later I realised why I had married him.

Let us go back to my teens. This man I had known my whole life. I remember the day of his mother's wedding, we snuck off outside the church hall and sat and spoke for what seemed like minutes, but it was hours. We even shared what felt like my first meaningful, gentle and loving kiss. We lost contact for many years, and I saw him again some years later at my auntie's. My belly flipped. Was it fear, excitement, or lust? I truly do not know. Nothing transpired, we spoke, and it was like he had always been in my life, and we had not lost contact.

I carried on with my life, got married, had two beautiful children, but unfortunately our marriage ended after fifteen years together. A story I have no need to share. Again, out of the blue, some fifteen years later, I received a message request on Facebook; it was him. I replied straight away and we sent messages back and forth all night long. A week later, he was at my door. My heart fluttered. I was single and a man I had aways thought about was standing there smiling. He threw his arms around me – oh those arms, so strong and warm. At that moment, I felt fantastic. I invited him in, and we laughed, we talked, and he reminded me so much of my childhood, visiting my auntie with my family and, of course, my dad.

Little did I know then he was suffering from depression, had a past I knew nothing about and was living in a flat that was uninhabitable. Nor did I know I was about to invite a monster into my home, my children's safe, loving home. We continued to talk and meet up. How could I not have seen his hidden agenda; the Hyde in my Dr Jekyll.

A month or so passed and he told me he had been made redundant and could not afford the rent on his flat. Well, that was just the first lie in a trail of them. I offered to help him sort out somewhere to stay, which would turn out to be the biggest mistake of my life.

I remember going to help him move out of his flat and I was shocked at the way he had been living. This should have rung alarm bells; unfortunately it didn't. I felt sorry for him. How could I go home to my beautiful house knowing he was living like this? So that's when I offered for him to stay with me and my children. After all, he was family.

We began a relationship a short time after that. He was kind, would undertake odd jobs around the home, help with the children, cook, clean and pay me some long-awaited attention. This went on for a few months, but it didn't last. BAM, out of nowhere, he began shouting and throwing things around the house. The phone shot past my ear like a torpedo; it was over nothing. I couldn't calm him down. He punched the patio door and I thought it would break. He stormed into the kitchen shouting foul abusive words at me from a distance. What could I do? I was stunned. I heard him on the phone talking to his sister. I knew later on that this was the only person he would never get angry at. I had already called the police. He started to come back into the house and I froze. He threw the phone at me and said, "Speak to my sister, you ★★★★!" She was so calm, why was she so calm? I was shaking like a leaf falling from an autumn tree.

"He'll be fine," she said. "He does this sometimes, don't worry, he'll be fine." She seemed so calm. I thought to myself, *Okay, she's calm, maybe I'm overreacting.* He spoke to her again for some time, came back in the house, hit the floor, crying, saying, "Sorry, please forgive me, I love you." Guess what? I forgave him and I dropped the charges.

But this behaviour continued escalating. He went through job after job after job. He always told the most elaborate stories, and yes, I believed them. I even found out later he had been fired from one job for punching his manager in the face. He stopped contributing to household bills, just lying around all day. He would snap at the children, making comments. Why is it words cut so deep inside? The verbal abuse was for me the most hurtful thing; not the violence and sexual abuse that came later, but the cruel words he would so easily string together.

I was walking on eggshells. I stopped seeing friends, family and the children were not allowed friends over to play. I kept quiet – smiles on the outside, the most unbearable pain on the inside. I let it continue. Why did I let this go on so long? Because I thought I could change him. I asked him to leave numerous times, but twenty-four hours later I would let him back in. Why? Because I thought I could change him.

On the final day, which I still remember so vividly, the children were at their father's, so I knew what was coming. It had got to the stage I would do anything to stop them going because this was the time he would become the monster I feared so much. This particular night, we had a lovely meal, watched some TV and went up to bed. He asked, "Why do you love me?" I paused… my mind went blank. Well, within a split second, he was on top of me with his hands around my throat, the anger in his eyes all I could see, his mouth moving but I could hear no words. Black… darkness… I remember a feeling of falling fast into darkness. He strangled me. No sound, no feeling, just utter darkness. I had passed out. I came round after he slapped my face so hard that I can still feel the stinging while writing this chapter.

He backed away and went downstairs. Some time passed, I really don't know how long. I needed to get out, how could I get out? I knew I couldn't, as every time we'd argued he had already hidden my phone and house keys, which was scary as it was all premeditated, something I had not even noticed until later. I just sat, stunned. I slowly went into another bedroom. He was in the garden. This was my opportunity, I could climb out of the downstairs window. The house phone was peeping out under a cushion, so I grabbed it and ran to the back door, locked it and called the police. He saw me, came running, shouting, punching the conservatory door. He kept saying he would kill me, kill my children and, at that moment, I believed it. He was livid. I just shook. The lady on the phone said they were nearly there and I should stay on the phone. That minute seemed like a lifetime. He had already called his sister and she arrived seconds after the police. He was arrested and statements were made. Social services were involved, and I had a long journey ahead. Although his sister and my mum knew most of the details of our relationship, I'd kept a lot to myself. I feared for my children's and my safety; I still believe to this day he would have killed me or my children.

I had called the police before. He was arrested this time but I dropped the charges; the main reason was the guilt of how this would affect my auntie, my family. I worried about people's opinions instead of the children I should have protected – the wrong choice, but I made it nonetheless. In the end, I had a choice whether to make this the final time he could cause harm to me or my children.

I attended a programme for victims of domestic abuse. It was a phenomenal course, I owe them my life. I began rebuilding my life day by day. It wasn't easy, but it can be done. You will smile again; you will find peace and feel safe.

The most painful part of this story was losing my son. I had chosen a violent, evil man over the feelings of my children; something for years I didn't forgive myself for. I know I have been judged, but I also know many women understand that you can't just get out – there are ways to leave safely, ways to learn how to live with domestic abuse and ways to forgive yourself. My son chose to live with his father, which was the most painful day of my life. The memory and pain of that day will never go, I truly believe that, but I have now forgiven myself. I am still unable to write about the night his father came to get him without feeling that heavy pain in my heart. My children deserve a mother who could give herself fully to them. I knew I had made the right decision. I could do this; I didn't need a man in my life.

I made the wrong choices and, in that process, I not only hurt myself, but I hurt my children, the ones I was supposed to love unconditionally, be a role model to and, most importantly, protect from harm. I failed. But I've since learnt that I stayed as I believed he would harm them if I left, and I still believe that. I learnt that part of holding on to this man was holding on to my dad, and my dad's side of the family. I have since attended grief counselling twenty-three years after my father had passed away. I have now grieved. I have delved into self-help groups, undertaken the most amazing programmes to better myself, to be a better parent, to be me.

Most of my learning has been around domestic abuse and self-healing. Many say violence stems from low self-esteem, stress, drink, being overworked or insecurity. The real reason for their violence and abuse is the desire to keep women under control. Violence isn't used every day. Some abusive men never need to use it at all because they can control us by other tactics. Violence normally arises if these other tactics are failing. I must say here that this goes for abusive female partners too. It's all about power, control, being dominant. They bully by using intimidation, shouting, sulking, firing question after question at you. Emotional abuse is used to put you down – you're ugly, you're fat – here is where you lose your self-confidence. By isolating you, stopping you seeing friends and family, this again is about control. Most lie, but they often lie to themselves, making their abuse seem less, followed by a string of excuses. Children are often used in domestic abuse as a bargaining chip, a threat, making you doubt your ability as a mother. It's all about control, using you as a servant, controlling money, and generally making all the major decisions. Sex is used to control you too, often leaving you feeling dirty, used and unable to stand up to them because they have ground you down. They are so persuasive, often coming into play after the relationship has ended. Remember, all our actions are motivated by our beliefs. The abuser holds hundreds of beliefs which allow them to abuse.

If we believe that all men are the same, we will tend to stay with them. We come to think this behaviour is normal. But think about this: if this was your son, would you want him to behave this way? What would you think?

I also learnt that no man is a saint, they are just decent human beings. We all want to be shown physical affection, but from someone who accepts it's your right to say no. We want a friend, someone to confide in and talk through any worries with. A man who welcomes your friends and family, who shares domestic responsibilities, is a good father, or stepfather. Someone who doesn't lie, and admits when they are wrong. Just a man who behaves like a reasonable human being. How would it feel to have a little confidence building in there too? A man who values your opinions, supports your dreams, aspirations, who values you for just being you.

The man I have described walked into my life over

two years ago. I posted something on Facebook. He sent a message and it said, "Hi, I saw your post, just seeing if you're okay?" At first, I opened it and thought, *Who is this guy? That's a bit random*. But nonetheless, I replied and said I was fine and automatically asked how he was. He replied with a kind, positive comment. End of conversation.

Hmmmmm… another message. Do I open it, do I ignore it? I certainly wasn't looking for a relationship. A few weeks later, I met him at his home for a coffee. That moment he came to the door, I was standing there in my uniform after a Covid nursing shift, I'll say no more. His eyes, they must be the most alluring, beautiful, loving eyes I have ever had the pleasure to meet. We sat, had coffee, and the eye contact was unbelievable. He was listening, yes listening to me, how weird was that? We continued to see each other, and our relationship blossomed. I had pushed this man away on several occasions, often letting him down: why? He was just too nice.

I was studying at the time and came across a quote:

"If you have been brutally broken, but still have the courage to be gentle to others then you deserve a love deeper than the ocean itself."

Nikita Gill

This was a turning point for me, even though I'd kept our relationship hidden for two years. It took me months to realise what this was. It was love, undoubtably the best love from a man I have ever felt. He accepted me, my past, my children,

25

and my illnesses. I chose to put up those barriers, to not show him love, but he could see something in me I could not see in myself. I didn't believe there would be anyone who would want to be with me. I deserved to be loved and felt ready to open that door, break down those walls.

He knows every aspect of my past and listened without judgement. He didn't want to change me and found the things I had to say interesting. He would delve deeper; he cared. He has the most caring heart. He is the opposite of the monster I once had in my life. He has supported the writing of this chapter. Starting a new relationship after an abusive one, for me, was easy and safe. I've not only learnt to love him but to love myself. He makes me feel trusted and respected in our relationship. We are now buying our first home together and it just feels so right. For me, it's the small things, the notes, saying to drive carefully, asking how my children are, offering to help in any way he can, running a bath for me, helping me shower when I'm in so much pain. He remembers when my prescription is due, what drug I take and what it's for. He cares. I feel loved, supported and have found my soulmate.

I am a strong believer that things happen in life for a reason. If I had not posted on Facebook that day, we may never have met. Had I not lived in a certain place, our paths would never have crossed.

It is possible to free yourself from an abusive relationship, to leave, to feel safe and to find love. I have made it my purpose in life to support as many women as I can to break free. To be you and to be loved.

★★★

In dedication to all the women currently living with domestic abuse in their lives; I see you. To all those women who have found the courage to break free, and rebuild their lives, I honour you. To my daughter Megan who has witnessed and held me together over the years; she has shown maturity and strength – I love you, you're my best friend. To my son Thomas for forgiving me for my mistakes and giving me a second chance to make right my wrongs, I thank you and I love you, I am so proud of you. My best friend Jason, who always finds the right words and never fails to make me smile, I love you, another rock in my life. To the special man in my life for being patient, for reminding me how to smile and laugh, for showing me that I need not fear love, and to take life by the hand and, of course, to dance in the rain, I thank you, I hear you and I love you. xxx

Ashleigh Quick is a mother of two beautiful children, a boy and a girl now aged eighteen and twenty, and is extremely proud of them both. Ashleigh qualified as a nurse in 1996, she then went on to study a degree and master's in oncology and palliative care. She has worked as a chemotherapy nurse specialist for over twenty-six years. During her spare time, she enjoys carp fishing, yoga, walking, reading and spending quiet time with her family. Ashleigh has always seen herself as an empath and strives to put others first. She thrives on learning new things and qualified as an NLP practitioner in 2020 and as a hypnosis practitioner and a meditation practitioner and teacher in 2022.

Ashleigh has always been passionate about helping others. She has a personal path to follow, helping women following a domestic abuse relationship, offering the tools they need to heal and move forward. She has a free Facebook group where she offers a different yet powerful approach to managing low self-esteem, boosting confidence by unveiling those doubts, and by offering a holistic approach. She also helps people with chronic pain and unwanted chemotherapy side effects. Ashleigh herself has been a chronic pain sufferer for many years and was shown the power of NLP and hypnosis to relieve symptoms. This led to her forming her own path to help others as she has been helped. She also assists families with the difficult task of talking to their children regarding life-limiting conditions and the potential outcome.

https://linktr.ee/ashleigh_hp

Listen to the audio version here:
https://bit.ly/Behindcloseddoors

SURVIVING LIFE AS A MOTHER OF TWINS

Heather Hulbert

"Being a mother of twins is a lesson about strengths you didn't know you had or dealing with fears you didn't know existed."

— *Linda Wooton*

Becoming a first-time mum to any child, let alone to twins or triplets, is a highly emotional and stressful time. You have no idea what you're doing, and neither does this wiggling ball of limbs in front of you either. Day or night? Who cares, let's just cry and sleep whenever we want to!

I want to share with you today my journey to becoming a parent, and, more specifically, a twin mum because I'm not going to lie, it's been an absolute bloody minefield navigating my way through the last four years. I spent a lot of time in the early stages of pregnancy hunting for blogs and YouTube videos of other twin mums, with the hope of finding little golden nuggets of advice to make my life easier. There are a lot of really good resources out there, and if I can help even just one person, I'll feel like this has been worth sharing.

As well as all the obvious good parts – having an extension of yourself to love unconditionally – motherhood is overwhelming, scary and exhausting, and what they don't prepare you for is how lonely it can be. So, I want to share my journey with you today in the hope that other mums in my situation will know they're not alone in feeling this way. Because that's exactly how I felt.

As a mum of multiples, it can feel like you're the only one who's ever done it before (even though you know full well that's not the case). When you first see those two blue lines on your pregnancy test, your life is instantly changed forever. You're filled with joy, excitement, and anticipation at all the possibilities that are going to be happening. You have visions of how your future self will look with your new family member, dreaming about what their nursery will look like, wondering if they will be a boy or girl, and maybe you even start thinking about names. From the moment the second line appears, you're a mother, way before your precious baby arrives.

Then you go for your scan, and you find out it is more than one. I'm not going to lie, when the sonographer said that there were two babies on screen, I actually told her to f★★★ off and just laughed. I was in complete and utter disbelief. I grabbed my husband's hand as he sat there staring at the screen, unmoving and silent.

All the plans in my head that I had been making suddenly all changed. After the initial shock and excitement came the overwhelm and anxiety. What did this mean for me and my pregnancy? Would it be safe? What are the added risks of having a twin birth versus a singleton? What kind of twins were they, because there are different types, and some come with more complications than others? Thankfully, for me, I had the 'safest' of the variations, so to speak, with each baby in their own amniotic sac and their own placenta, so we didn't have to worry about the risk of twin-to-twin transfusion syndrome (TTTS). This is where one baby ends up taking all the nutrients from the other baby, which can be life-threatening for one or either of the twins.

But all of a sudden, you're left thinking, 'Hang on a minute, how am I going to afford two children?' One child was going to be a stretch to pay for, now I had to think about getting two of everything! Two car seats, two cots, a double buggy (don't get me started on the price of those!), two sets of nursery fees, and a bigger car – I couldn't physically fit the babies, my buggy, and my husband in my car all at the same time! Yet another expense to have to plan for. Oh, and the amount of washing you're going to have to be doing, it suddenly takes all the fun out of the 'honeymoon' phase of your pregnancy. And then you end up feeling guilty because you should be excited and happy that this is happening and that you've been gifted with not just one child but two children, or more if you're having triplets or quads. Honestly, I take my hat off to anyone with multiple births more than twins because, I'm telling you now, it was hard enough with twins – at least they had an arm each and a boob each to feed from!

It feels like one thing after another. What is meant to be

a calm, enjoyable time looking forward to your new arrival is now filled with all this extra stress.

As the pregnancy went on, I ended up with symphysis pubis dysfunction (SPD) and severe back pain and I could barely walk unaided without crutches by the end of my pregnancy. Rather than being midwife-led the whole time, having regular check-ups and measuring your belly to see how the baby is growing, everything was way more clinical with the twins, as we had to be consultant-led, which meant I had many more appointments and additional growth scans to check everything was okay. Thankfully for me, it was.

Making an Entrance with a Bang

My twins were born on the first of January 2018. Talk about starting your New Year's resolutions off with a bang! I hadn't even had a chance to think of what I wanted for breakfast that day and, suddenly, I was having major surgery to give birth.

There's always a worry that you might end up having premature babies with a multiple birth. You're told stories of babies going into NICU, not coming home for weeks on end, and spending the majority of your precious maternity leave in hospital. But I want to reassure you that it's not always like that. There are many times when twins go to term (which is actually thirty-seven weeks for a twin pregnancy, rather than forty weeks) and come home within a day or two, just like a regular singleton birth.

For me, the positions they were in meant we had to have a caesarean section birth – all planned out down to the day we'd booked in. But, of course, they had other ideas and decided to give me a rude awakening at an ungodly hour on New Year's Day morning, ten days before their planned c-section. This meant that they were actually four weeks early and did need to go into the NICU, but it wasn't because they were poorly or needed any medical interventions, they were simply just on the small side at four and a half pounds each and needed help with feeding and regulating their temperatures for a few days.

We spent most of the time in the nursery on the neonatal ward, which is a much calmer area without all the hustle and bustle of incubators, monitors and alarms constantly going off. Don't get me wrong, it was the hardest twelve days I've ever had, on a constant three-hour cycle of changing, feeding, checking their NG tubes hadn't moved, breastfeeding to start them off before prepping their formula to tube-feed them. Before I knew it, I had a half-hour window before the whole cycle had to start again.

Coming Home

Looking after two babies is an absolute killer. All you want to do is get home to the place that you feel safe and are familiar with – your own home, your own creature comforts, your own bed.

I was in the recovery suite, happily eating my tea and toast, texting friends and family wishing them a Happy

New Year, oh and by the way, I've just had the twins! It wasn't until about four hours later that I got to even meet them. I was wheeled up to the NICU ward and promptly presented with one of my babies, handed the tiniest of bottles and asked if I wanted to give him a feed. I felt like a deer in the headlights. What's going on? I thought I was meant to have skin-to-skin and help them find their way to their first feed on me, that's what all the books tell you at least. It all felt very surreal, as if I was on the outside watching it happen to someone else (which was quite possibly the spinal block having an effect still as well). But I remember feeling out of control – these were my babies, but I was being dictated to as to where they went, when they would be fed, and how long we would stay in hospital. It felt like all the plans we had thought of had been thrown out of the window and there was me merrily thinking we might be in for just a couple of days. But then the first nurse we saw said, "Well, they might be here until their due date at the end of the month." Wait, what? You mean, I can't just take them home? Nothing quite prepares you for hearing those words. It's like the floor falling out from underneath your feet. This isn't the way it's supposed to be.

I spent many days and nights exhausted and in tears, wishing we could go home, praying the doctors would say today is the day, they've put on enough weight and you're okay to leave. Although I was free to leave myself, I felt trapped, almost imprisoned there with my babies. I didn't want to leave them, why would any mother want to do that? By day six I was told to go home and have a night off in my own bed. I was broken, and as much as it hurt to leave them, it was the right thing to do. The nurses were amazing and helped us out in so many ways you can't imagine; their kindness, knowledge and skills were second to none and I will be forever in their debt for giving us the support we needed before we started this journey called parenthood alone.

The Fourth Trimester

The first four months went by in a complete and utter blur; if I'm honest, I don't have much recollection of that time. Other than the obvious endless feed – change – sleep – repeat cycle and seeing photos and videos from those early weeks.

As many first-time mums often do, back when the twins were newborns, I started a blog with the aim to document the highs and lows of my journey, both as a first-time mum, and as a mum of twins. It was back in the days of hours spent sitting on the sofa under the feeding pillow, with my stash of snacks and drinks to hand, Netflix at the ready, and a lot of time on my hands to think and reflect… how times change!

I think this, along with a twin mum Instagram account, was more for my own sanity than anything else, to help keep my brain from turning into a complete zombified mush. Anything to keep a little bit of normality from your life pre-babies. Four years down the line and it's long been forgotten, sadly, but it's still nice to read back through from time to time. Even if no one else has ever read anything I posted, just giving myself something else to focus on that doesn't revolve entirely around the babies' routines was so important – a bit like your teenage Dear Diary days but for everyone on the internet to see.

School Days Are Coming

Now as I sit down and look back at how much the boys have changed over the first few years, the early newborn days feel like they happened a lifetime ago. I find myself mourning the 'easy' days where they just ate and slept (isn't hindsight a wonderful thing?). It certainly wasn't 'easy' when I was in the thick of it and just counting down the hours until bedtime every night, knowing I'd managed to survive another day, and dare I say it, even feeling a bit broody for another one… *maybe*?

That moment has definitely passed for me now. At around two to two and a half, I felt a real yearning for a second pregnancy. I'd always wanted two children, but a part of me felt like I had been cheated out of doing it again for a second time. Knowing I would never be pregnant again, or hold my newborn in my arms, smelling the sweet scent of their freshly washed hair – there's nothing quite like a newborn smell, is there? I felt guilty for even thinking about wanting to try again, and how that would affect the twins. Now, at four and a half, I know for sure that I'm finished with that part of my life. Finally, it's getting easier, they're way more independent now, they've always got a buddy to play with (and fight with as well, it's not all lollipops and roses!), but now we're about to start the next phase and start school, I can't imagine going back to those early days again.

Sleep Whenever You Can

Everyone tells you to sleep when the baby sleeps. Well, that's all well and good when you've got one baby (and sometimes not even then when they don't sleep very well). What happens when you've got two? How do you manage to sleep then? Surely they're going to be constantly feeding, and one or the other will be needing you all the time, so how do you stop the guilt when you're dealing with one baby and the other one is screaming his little lungs out to get your attention too? The answer is that you can't always deal with both at the same time, and as hard as it is to hear them crying, it's okay for them to wait a few minutes.

The biggest piece of advice I was ever given that I want to pass on to any new twin mums reading this is to get them in a routine as early as possible, and I know that's not always easy with babies. They're the ones who dictate when they're hungry, when they're sleepy, when they decide to empty their nappy at the most inconvenient times. But, in the first six to eight weeks, teach them if one has been changed, the other one gets changed too; if one baby wakes in the night to feed, wake the other one up as well. They will soon pick up on the cues that it's time for milk or naps, etc., and this is the only way you'll be able to get any kind of breather to have a sleep yourself, or even just make yourself a hot cuppa and have a break from holding a baby 24/7. If you're breastfeeding, make sure you invest in a decent tandem pillow – it will be a life saver on your back. Even now, my twins are still very much in sync with each other, and I strongly believe that's from pushing through in those early days.

Four o'clock was always the worst time for us. We nicknamed it the witching hour. It's when you'll be at your most tired because you've been up in the night to feed, you've been up all day and you're just waiting for your partner to come home from work so you can pass them over to have a shower. I would often text my mum to make sure she was going to pop in after work to help me out. They say it takes a village to raise a child, and with twins that's even more true. I would not have got through the early months if it hadn't been for the support network I had around me, taking the babies for a cuddle or a feed so I could freshen up. The days are long when you're on your own. It seems mad to think that with two babies to keep you busy how could you possibly get lonely, but you really do.

Luckily for me, one of my friends was also having a baby at the same time and had formed a friendship with her NCT group of mums. NCT isn't something I had done myself, so being accepted into their tribe was the best thing that could've happened. Find your tribe so that when you're going through the hard days, you know it's not just you.

There are days when you really don't want to get out of the house, but you know that you need a change of scenery, even if that's just a trip to your local supermarket to wander around the aisles aimlessly. Of all the days I forced myself to get dressed and go out, I never once regretted it.

Playdates are a godsend, even if you don't actually get to leave the house. You know those friends where you can just rock up in whatever you're wearing, not having to make an effort and get dressed up? It's a case of turning up, putting the baby on the floor in the jungle gym, making yourself a hot cup of tea and having someone else to talk to. But it can still be such a lonely experience doing this with friends who aren't in the same situation you're currently in.

I remember going to meet some friends who I hadn't seen in months when the twins were about eleven months old. One had just had a baby herself and, although it was lovely to see them, I felt such a disconnect with them. It was like they were from a previous life now. I couldn't have a proper conversation with any of them as I had to have eyes in the back of my head, watching them to make sure they didn't do anything stupid like putting tiny toys in their mouths. I may as well have just been sitting at home for the amount of conversation I actually had with my friends. I came away from that meet-up feeling like it was a complete waste of time and feeling so incredibly lonely that I cried on the drive home. I felt like I'd lost that connection to who I was before I became a mum. People would say to me, "I bet you can't imagine life without them, can you?" And the truth is, I could in those early days. There were days when I felt a disconnect with them; I was just going through the motions from the moment I woke up to the moment we put them to bed. And it feels awful to admit that, but it's true.

Double the Fun, But Double the Expense!

Being a mum of any kind has its challenges; being a twin mum brings not just double the challenges, but quadruple. There are the costs of everything you need to buy, from all the extra nappies and the food to the clothes and the baby classes. You're lucky if you get a 10% discount for the second child, and that's all well and good if you've got children of different ages, you expect to pay for them individually. But I'd been blessed enough to have them together, and for the most part, baby groups are more for the parents than the children, to give them a change of scenery for an hour or two. I don't think I managed to massage either of the twins properly in a single class of baby massage during the whole six weeks I attended! So, to have to pay out twice for classes like that limited my choices of what we could do together being only on statutory maternity pay. The class we chose for baby massage only charged per parent, which was a lifesaver. I couldn't go swimming with them whenever I wanted, I had to wait until my husband or my mum could come with me to help. It's not fun holding two slippery eels, trying not to drown them!

Loneliness was by far the biggest thing I struggled with. You might wonder how you can be lonely when you've got two children who need your attention 24/7. You can have friends and family all around you all the time, helping out, and be in a room full of people and yet still be lonely. No one prepares you for that emptiness you feel in the pit of your stomach when you go on a play date to the park and all the other children of the same age are off running around having fun, and your children are still only crawling, leaving you sitting on the picnic blanket just watching the fun happen around you. I always felt like we were one step behind everyone else. It doesn't matter how much you tell yourself its okay, that every child develops at their own rate, when you see all your friends around you moving on to the next step before you, it does feel so isolating.

There were several occasions when group events had been arranged and I just didn't feel, logistically, like I could go. So, then you're back to feeling stuck and lonely again. But honestly, it does get better. And that's the message I want to give to other mums in the same situation as me. Mine are now four going on five. They're starting school in a few months, and they literally cannot wait to go. Truth be told, neither can I! They are so ready for the next adventure.

I'd always wanted to have children, and I'm so grateful that I have been blessed with two amazing, funny, kind little boys, it really does make all the hard times so worth it.

Nowadays I can actually go to a friend's house and take the boys, let them run loose and play, have a hot cup of coffee and an actual catch-up with a friend. And it's bliss!

It's taken four years to get to that place but I'm so grateful that things do change. They do get easier, so hold onto that hope and you'll get through the darker days.

★★★

Dedicated to Leo and Oliver – the lights of my life. Without you, the days would be a lot darker. Thank you for showing me what it means to love unconditionally.

I'd also like to dedicate this to all the multiple mums out there who are struggling. This is your reminder that you are doing an incredible job and there are brighter days ahead for you.

Heather is a mum of four-year-old twin boys. She's also a branding and website designer with over twenty years of experience. She specialises in helping female entrepreneurs by taking the stress and overwhelm out of the tech in their business and making sure their branding

and online presence truly represents their personality, their values and their vision for the future, in a genuine and authentic way.

https://heatherhulbert.co.uk/connect

Listen to the audio version here:
https://bit.ly/SurvivingLifeasaMotherofTwins

INFIDELITY AND HOW TO SELF-CARE YOUR SURVIVAL THROUGH TO THE OTHER SIDE

Audrey Stewart

> *"A thought is just a thought, and a thought can be changed. I am not limited by past thinking. I choose my thoughts with care. I constantly have new insights and new ways of looking at my world. I am willing to change and grow."*
>
> – *Louise Hay*

On the 26th of December 2004, my phone rang. I answered it, and a male voice on the other side said the following words to me: "This is Peet. I just called to tell you that your husband has been f*cking my wife." Then the line went dead. To this day, nearly the eighteenth anniversary, these words are burned into my brain and my psyche.

That date might ring a bell for you, as it was also the date of the tsunami in Indonesia, the deadliest in recorded history. In my own life, there was a tsunami of wave after wave of emotions that were threatening to overwhelm and drown me.

If you are reading this and that "bombshell" has hit

your life in one way or another, all I can say is that I am so sorry that this has happened to you. I hold this space for you, knowing that you are not alone in what you are feeling and going through. However, if I can make it, so can you.

If unicorns and fairy dust are what you are looking for then this is not the place for you. Neither will anything suggested here be energetic bypassing, as none of that will help, and will most likely only prolong your discomfort, as the last eighteen years – including a second affair – have taught me. That is why I am here to be a beacon of hope and light for you.

Now, I am not going to give you advice as to what you need to do about your situation. For that you will need to follow your heart. From experience, following your heart may be very challenging, as due to the shock your heart (energetic heart – chakra) may have closed partially or completely, thus making it difficult to even access your heart, let alone make decisions from this place. Please keep reading as I will include tips on how to work with this.

The "E" word is almost as scary as the "F" word. Just remember that emotions will come, most likely in waves. It's okay and even if it isn't right now, it will be. Remember this: Emotions are "E"nergy in MOTION. Feel them. Sit with them. Cry, scream, punch your pillow, do all those things, repeatedly if you have to. Allow the emotions to flow through you and do your best not to hold on to them. Acknowledge each and every one as it makes its appearance. Once they start to become less intense, take some time to sit quietly and with no distractions and see if you can ask each one what the lesson is that it brings into your life. It would help to have a pen and journal available, so that you are able to note down what comes up for you. Really listen to that little voice inside, the internal prompts that will come up are the nuggets of a lesson. If you take the perspective that everything in your life has a lesson to teach you, then ask yourself what that would be? Yes, this will be really hard to do, but isn't everything that is worthwhile doing outside of your comfort zone?

Some of the journal prompts that I used were as follows:

- What was good about this time?
- What was bad about this time?
- Did you learn anything about yourself?
- Did you remember anything that you had forgotten?
- What were your wins?
- What showed strength, tenacity and courage?
- What were your moments of joy and happiness?
- What were your challenges?
- What were the gifts?
- What do you need to release?
- What didn't work out?
- How might you have contributed?
- What do you need to forgive, let go of or release as part of this process of beginning a new cycle?
- What do you need to renew?
- What do you do really well?
- What about yourself can you celebrate?
- How have you contributed to your wins and moments of success and happiness?

- What are the common ingredients of your joy in the last month/year/decade?
- Look for the feelings/situations and ask yourself how you can duplicate these moving forward.

Once this is done and out of your system, start building a picture of what you do want. Start a NEW story. Focus on what you would want it to look like. How would you like it to play out? This may be really challenging to do; I know that I struggled to do this for a long time. Take heart, this is possible, and things will get better. Take responsibility for your thoughts as quickly as you can, as where your thoughts go, the energy flows. Thoughts are magnetic and they have frequency as well. Make an extra effort to be conscious of what you think because thought is directing energy. What you send out, you get back three-fold. I say this not to scare you, but to raise your awareness of it.

When you journal, imagine all these emotions and thoughts (mind monkeys) are flowing energetically down your arm and out of the pen onto the paper. This is a vital part of the process, as the more that you drag this around with you, the more vibrational resistance you are creating, which will block what you do want, as it is still in vibrational resonance with what has happened, and none of us want to go back there. Make that decision; for me it is the reminder phrase of "back is not an option". More on this a bit later. Bottom line is that all of this that is coming out is still in alignment/frequency with the old wounds, and that is not what we want in our lives.

On the more practical side, take care of everyday life. Yes, you heard me, get up out of that bed, and your PJs. Take a shower or a bath, get dressed into something that makes you feel good, do your hair, have a proper meal, tend to your family, fur babies, or whomever else is in your life. Do it now if you haven't already. Go for walks in nature, visit the seaside and put your feet in the water. Exercise in whichever format is good for you, as the physical movement helps you move that energy through your body. Play your favourite music out loud every day. Pick the songs that make you feel happy, though. Elton John's 'I'm Still Standing' is one of my go-to songs.

Get help for everyday life. Yes, order in, get takeout, use ready meals, ask a friend to cook, do all of those things if you can. Pay the bills, do the washing, put petrol in your car. Go to work. Take care of the daily everyday things and keep doing it. These are your connections to sanity, no matter how bizarre or mundane this will feel. The fact is that no matter how broken you are feeling right now, the world will keep turning, the sun will rise in the morning.

For all of you with a joint bank account, if you don't already have one, open a bank account in your own name. Put some money in it. This is for you. Don't tell them about this either. If you are working, get your salary paid into this account first. This gives you the control over your money. If you aren't working, find a job, something to get you out of the house. For me this meant formally completing my executive assistant training, hard as that was in the middle of the 2020 lockdown – literally locked in with the person

I was struggling to like, never mind the fact that he was actually my husband. Struggling with processing my own emotions and stretching myself to formalise my skills was probably one of the toughest things I have done in my life. It was, however, worth every bit of blood, sweat and tears, as the sense of achievement when completed gave my sense of self-worth a much-needed boost. The job that I secured was the best acknowledgement of that achievement ever.

Seek professional help. Yes, speak to parents and the like if you are fortunate to have them in your life, but most importantly, seek professional help. My best advice is to avoid discussing the events with all and sundry, as not all will be as supportive as you might have hoped. Having the people around you taking sides is NOT helpful. I made that mistake, and he had his family all jumping on him with reprimands and the like. This did not help, as part of the issue that was in play was his own lack of sense of self.

Journal in whatever format works for you but keep it private. Write down everything that is flowing through you without filters or censorship. If you are finding this too overwhelming, try the following: imagine the scene in front of you, but from a faraway perspective, so climb a tree if you must, to keep the observer status. Make the scene black and white and very small, like a movie on a tiny screen. Even make the people speak with squeaky voices to remove the emotional charge from this. Watch it, but keep yourself detached, and process it from as many perspectives as you can as many times as you need to, until it doesn't come up for you.

I printed pictures that were posted on Facebook to rub the affair in my face – very small and in black and white – and stuck them into my journal in a form of collage with the question: *what is important about this time?* It took me a really long while, and then my inner voice told me the following: *"Karma. Sometimes there are things playing out that you just need to let play out. There are things we cannot control. There are certain people and situations that you cannot change and sometimes you have to accept that. I am moving out of emotion and ground and love myself. I step out and away from this and choose to give it no further emotional energy. I stay logical and strong and removed from the emotion of this situation. I choose my own peace and well-being, life force and relationships instead."* In a nutshell: I take my power back.

Another thing to try is to write an "unsent" letter that you address directly to a person. Write it all out, no filters, no censorship, no limits. Let it all flow as I have described above. Once this is done and you feel like you are "lighter" and have unburdened yourself, burn it. Safely, of course, either in a fireplace, or in a bowl in a safe space where you won't set your world or yourself alight. Preferably, outside – best of all as part of a full moon ceremony. While the letter is burning, imagine that the flames are transmuting all that heavy emotional energy that flowed and is stored in the words on the paper into golden light that rises up to the moon, to be transmuted and recycled by the universe.

Whilst I am giving advice, please avoid at all costs the social media type of breakups. Don't burn their clothes or pile them in the street. Don't paint CHEATER on their car. It might feel great in the short term, and publicly humiliating them might make you feel good in the moment, but it is really not worth it. Besides, this is firmly in the resonance of what you do not want in your life, don't focus there. Make a conscious effort to redirect your thoughts away from that which you don't want in your life. Yes, thoughts will come up and will often return, however it does not help you to give them any energy. Instead, find a way to redirect your energy to what you do want more of in your life.

You have a choice! This is a very important point, and I feel guided to elaborate a little bit more. From experience, in traumatic situations like this, the ego (that nasty voice inside) and the monkey mind like to rule the show, and this is the not-so-pretty side of ourselves that also needs to be embraced. This can be really hard work, but you have a CHOICE in this. You need to take responsibility for your thoughts and the perspective that you take. You can choose to be the victim, and yes this is a phase in processing what happened, but the choice is to acknowledge and process as best you can what comes up for you. We are all different and each of our life situations are different; however, there is also a commonality in our humanness. This is why I said at the start, the emotions will come, that is part of being human in this world, you need to know that they are here for you to experience and allow them as energy to flow through you. Now for the important bit that often gets missed. If you don't process and acknowledge what comes up, and you push it down or away and refuse to deal with them, that is how you create the shadow (dark – because you haven't allowed the light in). This shadow aspect of yourself becomes hard work. It will keep you stuck, as it is a lesson that you have refused to learn. Bearing in mind that what you resist persists, until you face those shadow aspects, which happens the moment you accept that you feel that way, with no judgement, and see, accept and learn the lessons. These may be to value yourself better, or to not accept behaviour that is destructive because you want to keep the peace, or you are afraid of being alone. While the most common reaction to infidelity is to leave that relationship, it doesn't mean that the lesson that is there for you is learnt. All it means is that you have moved away from that particular situation, but since the lessons are still there, you have seen the patterns of people who move onto another relationship, only to find themselves in the same or similar situation. Wash, rinse, repeat. You will hear the words "why does this keep happening to me?" Not to be harsh or anything, that is not my intention, but you need to process this and take the lessons onboard. You need to do your work. This is probably one of the hardest parts of the process, but it doesn't need to be. I had no idea that this was what I was meant to do with what had happened. My "sh★t cart" of life got really heavy and I was struggling in a big way. All credit goes to Kate Spencer and her Life and Soul Academy, who got me to realise these things and helped me find a way that worked for me. You have a choice, on the thoughts that you choose to think, and the meaning that you choose to give things. In the words of

Louise Hay, "A thought is just a thought, and a thought can be changed. I am not limited by past thinking. I CHOOSE MY THOUGHTS WITH CARE. I constantly have new insights and new ways of looking at my world. I am willing to change and grow."

If it resonates with you, I sincerely recommend getting in contact with an EFT practitioner. Tapping works as it removes the emotional charge behind all the memories and changes them back into the "mundane", which was what saved my life – to such a degree, I have chosen to study this and qualify as a level two practitioner. This is a journey that I would hesitate to wish upon my worst enemies, since they were the mistresses in his life, but I came out the other end so much stronger and in my power.

Lastly, expressions like "once a cheater, always a cheater" are in my eyes too general, and as such unfair. There are always factors in play that underpin the decisions made. Being the person that I am, I have always done my best to see and understand others' perspectives. If writing about my journey, hard as it was, has helped you in any way, then I feel that it was worth the journey. I wish you all the healing and light along your path. I feel blessed and honoured for any small part I may be able to play in your journey. Whilst I cannot ease your pain, my hope is that I am able to point you in a direction that will help you to find the healing you need.

***

To my younger self

Audrey is a wife, mother and so much more. She trained as a primary school teacher and has also run a business consultancy in South Africa. In 2009, she decided to relocate her family to the UK. With £2,000 in her pocket, she boarded a flight to the UK with her family. In 2015, she completed her level one in bio-energy healing, and level two in 2016. In 2020, she decided to venture out into the world of employment and qualified as an executive assistant. With this as her mundane job, she furthered her "energy" studies and is completing level two emotional freedom technique studies. As with everyone, there is far more to this journey than what meets the eye, and she hopes that the lessons she learned will act as a beacon for you in dark times. You can and will get through this, there is hope on the other side.

https://linktr.ee/audstew

Listen to the audio version here:
https://bit.ly/InfidelityandhowtoSelfCare

UNCONSCIOUSLY CHANGING AND HEALING GENERATIONAL PAIN

Kari Roberts

"I am not here to be right, I am here to get it right."
– Brené Brown

Thirty-eight years ago, I was told by the doctor I was pregnant. I was twenty years old, in a stable relationship, we'd just bought our home together with plans of remodelling, exotic holidays and fast cars ahead of us. My career was growing and I finally felt like I was flying. I fiercely questioned the doctor's diagnosis of the sickness and lethargy I had been feeling for four weeks and the fact that mother nature had not changed. So, in my mind, this was a bug! He was adamant there was no mistake! Immediately, I felt total surprise followed by a whole lot of fear. Even after the excitement started to creep in because, deep down, I had always wanted to be a mum, the legacy of the way I had been parented scared the pants off me. My pregnancy went well, I had one blip at twenty-six weeks, and I remember all my fears disappearing once I got through that. My inner voice just said, 'Well, it's going to happen, no turning back.' Finally, on the 20th of March

1985, I met my firstborn, my son. I had attended all the prenatal classes, learnt what would happen to me physically and lots of tips for breathing. No mention of parenthood and the feelings, emotions and loss of self this would evoke. I remember the huge rush of love I felt as he was born and wanting to never let him down. The hope of being a good mum to him flooded me. I was officially a MOTHER, but all the fears of what type of parent I was going to be filled my whole self. My fear of being like my mum. What if my children don't feel loved? Can I do this?

That day, looking into the eyes of my newborn son, I made him a promise. I would never hit him. Without realising it, I unconsciously broke a generational cycle of violence. I remember sitting on the stairs one day sobbing when he was three months old. He was in his cot crying. I had changed him, fed him and tried to comfort him. Nothing worked and, as I got more stressed, he got more and more worked up. I could feel the annoyance and frustration building inside me, but knowing I had to leave him in his cot for his own sake because of the fear bubbling up in me that I would lash out was heartbreaking. One of my biggest fears was that once I started hitting, I would not be able to stop. There was a sort of red rage that my mum had and, once she started hitting, she wouldn't stop, going beyond the point of reasoning. Often it was only through someone else saying "STOP" or her exhausting herself it would end. Remember when I made this decision not to hit my children, it was thirty-eight years ago and lots of my family and some friends didn't understand and would tell me I was going to spoil him. I didn't have the confidence to tell them the reasoning behind my why. There was so much shame attached to not having that confidence, as it meant opening myself up to being told I was silly for feeling that way or even worse being told I deserved all that had happened.

You see, I remember my childhood being one where I constantly lived in fear of being beaten. Living in bewilderment of never knowing when or why and feeling resentment towards the adults around me, especially my mother. Technically I was always in fight or flight mode and had years of just freezing my emotions because, every time I showed them, I was either ridiculed or beaten. My memory bank was filled with very unsafe memories, ones of coldness and violence. Memories of not fitting in anywhere, at home, at school or in society and so much emotional pain. My earliest memories were of a house with our bedroom leading off through another in Gosport, Hampshire. Being hit repeatedly because my sister and I were playing and making too much noise while we jumped on the bed. I think I was five. I went into school the next day and showed my teacher the marks on my legs. I was asked, "What did you do to upset your mother?"

When I was around seven, my parents had a very messy divorce, which was after my mother walked out one day leaving my sister and I with my father and was one of the happiest times I can remember. Not feeling scared to walk through the front door after school when she wasn't there. Always wondering what mood she was in and always walking on eggshells. I guess not having to keep quiet, not play and dodge beatings were nothing to miss. Then Mum turned up, and turbulence came when she returned to 'claim' us. Lots of fear, darkness and these butterflies in my tummy that made it hurt. My sister and I had to move away from the house I knew as home, the school I went to and the dad I felt safe with. There was a huge sense of loss. I don't remember but my sister reminds me often that it was because I was asked who I wanted to live with, and I said my mum. So, the narrative I had at that early age was that it was my fault and I deserved the beatings. I became an expert at self-sabotage. Wondering what I had done that was so bad. Starting a new school where I would stay in class with the teacher so I didn't have to go out to play and always feeling so alone. Even though my dad was heartbroken, he would turn up every weekend with a smile and I would feel so safe with him. But when we got back to my mum's I would cry because I didn't want him to leave and would cling to him. I can still remember my mum being so angry because she saw this as rejection. One time, she grabbed me as Dad put me down to talk to me and threw me in the house, slammed the door and left me sobbing in a ball where I eventually fell asleep. Little did I know that was the last time I would see him for nearly twelve years. Others have told me my dad was kind and loving and a decent man. The next day we boarded a plane and returned to the country of my birth, Malaysia. The courts had made us a ward of court as there was a risk Mum would take us out of the country. To this day, I do not know how she was able to leave with us.

Picture me as a seven-year-old child, running through the airport. It had been a long time since I had seen my stepdad. When my dad was stationed in Malaysia, he'd been a family friend, and my godfather. When my mother left my father, she got back in touch with him and they started their relationship. My mum had hyped up the excitement of moving back to Malaysia and how wonderful our life would be. I caught sight of him coming out of customs into the airport lounge and I ran to hug him. Running towards him, not seeing anything else, nearly being knocked over by another passenger pushing a trolley, I tripped and fell on the floor. Feeling devastated, embarrassed and hurt! Looking up to the two people I loved, my stepdad and my mum, who had caught up with me. Expecting a hug and concern that I was hurt. Instead, being told off and smacked for running, for not watching where I was going! What I needed at that time was to feel loved and connected to my parents. I grew up believing that you have to keep your emotions small and being spontaneous is something that is not acceptable. My sister bore the brunt of being older, having a rebellious spirit to challenge my mother, being brave enough to run and lock herself in the bathroom. I can remember when we lived in a wonderful house with an amazing staircase that overlooked the lounge. Mum was repeatedly hitting me, and my sister shouted over the banister, "You're mad, you're mad!" Mum stopped and chased after her. This was the only thing that stopped her from continuing to hit me. The red rage always came over her.

I always believed it was my fault, that if I was good

and did everything I was told, didn't fight back, didn't argue, then she would love me and not get angry. My inner narrative told me I was irresponsible, I was bad, I was not good enough to be loved. To add to my inner voice, I was in a position of being a minority. I was white in a predominantly mixed ethnic country. I was a bit of a novelty at school. The only white girl in my class and my sister and I were the only two in the whole school. We were not wealthy as most expats working in Malaysia were. My stepfather was in the Malaysian navy and paid the local rate, not inflated British naval pay. I searched for acceptance. This is where now I can see the need to get my needs met. As a child, I became very compliant very early on. Some children use humour, making everyone laugh, breaking the ice, some children use rescuing tactics, taking the blame, always keeping the peace, others use rebellion. My father was this light within me for many of my childhood years. All my memories of him as a child were warm, calm and safe. I loved fairy tales and reading was my escape. I felt hope for the future in these stories. Lying in bed, crying every night and then dreaming Dad would turn up and rescue me. My knight in shining armour, who rode in on a shining white horse and rescued me. This happened right up until I was fifteen; then I met a boy. I was very immature and, in my daydreaming, he took the place of my knight in shining armour. It crushed me when this relationship ended. It took me years later to realise that the only person who could rescue me was me.

During this time, I became very conscious of my size.

Everyone around me was small, more petite. Already having very low self-esteem, I believed that being smaller was the way to fit in. My boyfriend's sister mentioned it a couple of times. I found an article in a magazine that talked about bulimia – binge eating and then making yourself purposely vomit. My mindset of if there was nothing staying in my body then I would lose weight was flicked on. The rounds of bingeing and purging started. This was confirmed as everyone complimented me on losing weight and how good I looked. I finally thought I had found the magic answer to fitting in. But, of course, it soon became part of the self-loathing and fear that if I stopped doing it and put on weight, I would not be accepted.

When I was seventeen, I had a dream of a knight in armour standing in front of a mirror, lifting the lid of the helmet and the person staring back at me was not my father, it was me! This was when I stopped reducing myself, started to love myself and started to heal.

The promise I made not to hit my children was kept for sixteen years. I had two other children who were eleven and ten. My eldest was a teenager, he played basketball and his dream since the age of five was to go to and play in America, which had come true. He was due to leave in a couple of days and he wanted to go out with his friends, but I wanted him to stay home and have a family dinner. We started arguing. Ironically at this time I was supporting young people with their emotions as part of a health initiative. I was very emotional, and it was getting really heated, when he said to me, "Go on, I know you want to hit me, go on!" This is one of the lowest moments in my parenting. In my high emotional state, I hit him across the face! I am not sure who was more surprised by this, him or me. I felt so ashamed. I fell to the floor crying and he left in shock, but he soon came home to apologise and I told him how sorry I was. Thankfully, by then, I had started the process of healing myself and was able to be vulnerable and honest with him. In return, he was able to be honest with me with both of us being able to let go of the guilt. I am very proud of my children and the strong bond I have with all of them.

Growing up, one of the hardest things for me was feeling guilty for not feeling love for my mother and always living with the hope she would one day say sorry and change. Years later, I realised it was not that I didn't love her, it was that I didn't like her. All around me, people would say there is nothing like a mother's love, respect, honour and cherish your mums! This was not how I felt, and again I kept it hidden because I believed it was me, my fault and at one point truly thought I was evil! When I became a mother, I started to wonder more and more about her. I wanted to try to understand her more and let go of my childhood experiences and move forward. I had this inner push as I was tired of holding on to hate, shame and guilt. I knew for me to heal I had to forgive.

She was born to a very young mother and older father. Her mother was very pretty, and her dad was a gambler. My mum was conceived out of wedlock and, in those days – we are talking over ninety years ago – marriage or adoption were the two options. My grandmother was very resentful as she felt her life had been ruined. She wanted to party and go out but had to marry my grandfather. My mother was called a bastard from the day she was born; she always loathed that word, and it would visibly trigger her. Mum didn't understand why her parents kept her until she was in her eighties and found out about her father's first marriage and the death of his wife and twins. She then understood why they had not agreed to adoption. Mum had a brutal childhood, beatings, lack of love and warmth, not allowed treats, not going to school and working on the farm, having two fingers severed by a harvester machine before her fifteenth birthday. I remember my mother saying that she would be working with her father all day, coming back to the house with him, her mother blaming her for something and even though her father knew it wasn't possible she was to blame, taking his belt off and beating her! Her father also drank a lot and gambled most of their wealth away. Mum married young to flee the abuse but her first husband abused her. She was always terrified of water because he tried to drown her while her mother watched. When I think of my mum's experiences, it breaks my heart, and I am filled with deep compassion and understanding. She then met my dad. She had no trust, no worth and no idea how to show love and this is when I switched feelings of anger and resentment and let the love flood in. She was, however, deeply loyal and looked after her dad while he was dying of cancer. Deep down, she had so much compassion. There are so many people who will not believe this side of my mother. To others, she was charitable, caring, and went out of her way to help and support others. That was how she got her needs met. Sadly, she never found the peace I did and would not explore her healing. For her, it was safer to keep anger rather than let go of it. My mother did not have the capacity to forgive and the trauma she experienced was the cause of this. I know it's a cliché, but honestly, forgiving my mum was life changing for me.

I am now fifty-eight years old and the sadness that it took me over forty years to feel good enough sometimes catches me. Up until I was over forty, I worried about what people thought of me. How I looked, how I needed to play small and be physically small. I would spend endless hours worrying about things I had said or done. The freedom of stretching myself and realising that I could only control what I said and what I did was immense. It wasn't easy and there are still times I catch myself, but it passes quickly. That doesn't mean I say whatever I want and am not mindful of people's feelings, it just means I don't beat myself up over every action or word. There has always been an inner voice, something inside me has not allowed me to look negatively at the world or be a victim of my childhood. Some call it resilience, I call it my inner wisdom, the knowledge I am enough and have been since the day I was born. Every morning, I wake up saying thank you and, every evening, I go to bed saying the same thing. In a world where there is so little hope, I know how important hope is as, without that, I would have been lost years ago.

★★★

This chapter is dedicated to my mother for teaching me so much about myself and forgiveness.

Kari is a specialist parent coach. She works to build parents' confidence to parent in the way that works for them and their children, without breaking anyone's spirit. With over fifteen years of professional and thirty-seven years of personal experience as a mum to three and grandmother to nine, she knows that what children need is for the adults around them to be secure in who they are and be emotionally healthy. Start with you and then things for your children will fall into place!

https://linktr.ee/kariann2309

Listen to the audio version here:
https://bit.ly/ChangingGenerationalPain

I NEEDED HELP BUT MY SON NEEDED IT MORE

Candy Fung

'Everything happens for a reason – whether it's good or bad, you learn from it.'

My parents are from Hong Kong. I was born and raised in London, and have amazing teenage twin boys whom I raised as a single parent in Bromley, Kent, UK since they were five years old. After my parents divorced when I was nine years old, my brother and I had to learn how to be independent very quickly as Dad had custody of us, but he worked long hours in a restaurant. For secondary education, we went to boarding school (and had the best time). Growing up, we did not have parents around to guide us or look after us. Praise – what's that? Well done – for what? I guess that's why we're both so laid back and resilient when it comes to everyday life. Taking each day as it comes was what we did well. We adapted; we had to. We always did what we thought was right. We managed, we turned out okay.

I grew up with the man of my dreams, lived a wonderful life, got married and had twin boys – how priorities in life changed (for me)! I always knew we were different, so when he 'didn't want to be married anymore' I was not surprised. I cried the first night and then realised it was the best thing. For a while, I used to wonder why we didn't get on like other couples. I put it down to being together for so long (twenty-three years on and off to be exact). Little did I know, it would be the start of me finding happiness. I am aware I was stuck!

Back in 2005, I thought I was doing the right thing, bringing up my boys while my husband went out to work. He wanted me to be a stay-at-home-mum who 'did nothing'. I had no goal, no motivation, no purpose. I'd take each day as it comes. I could have and do whatever I wanted, as long as our boys were well fed and looked after. We were lucky enough to have at least three holidays a year. Of course, it seemed like a great lifestyle at the time – to be a 'lady of leisure'. I knew I wanted to do more but didn't know what or even have a reason, energy or the enthusiasm. That's when my life was at a standstill! Or, as the motivational speaker Tony Robbins would say, I was 'in no man's land, neither happy nor unhappy'… until my boys started school full-time. I started volunteering as a parent helper. I loved it so much, I enrolled on a teaching assistant course… best decision I made!

Why was I often feeling I was not enough? It came to me years later when I had an 'aha' moment that it was because my ex-husband used to put me down all the time. Of course, I know now that it was not all me with the issues. No wonder my life stood still for so many years. He was controlling and I didn't even see it at the time. I just knew we had nothing in common, we lacked communication (communication is KEY for me now), he wasn't interested in the day-to-day stories unless it involved him, we had different friends and lived separate lives.

When we had our twin boys, life changed, I changed. He hadn't changed (he even bragged 'the best thing about being a parent is it doesn't change anything'... errr, it should!). Parenting is scary as it is, without an instruction manual. We did whatever worked for us. I was never one to follow what the latest parenting books advised. However, what I did notice was that whilst I was loving being a new mum, admittedly it was stressful but happy stress. Their dad did not see it that way at all. The sleepless nights, the washing, the feeding, the chores (luckily, part of the Chinese tradition of having to stay home for one month, my mum was visiting every day to cook nutritious meals and helped wherever she could). Although he was great at doing exactly what I had asked and provided for us, the thing he lacked was patience (very testing for new parents). I understand that it can be quite frustrating when a baby cries. But one would cry more than the other. Any bad behaviour is a sign of an unmet need, right? So, why then did his dad say things like, "Shut the F★★★ up!" or, "What now?" Sleep deprivation is not good for anyone but he was a baby, we were adults. As the boys got older, one was favoured more than the other, who was often told 'no', 'you're so stupid', 'you're rubbish', 'don't do that', ' how can you not read?' The list goes on.

There used to be days when the boys had to literally

beg their dad to play in the garden with them. Then, when he finally went out, it was for ten minutes (reluctantly). It got to the stage where I had to record what he was doing, although that didn't change anything as he thought he was always right.

Answering the phone on loudspeaker was the one thing that could not be mistaken – depending on who answered the call, it would be either a cheerful, 'Hi son, how are you? What are you doing? Did you have a nice day?' or a monotone, 'Hello, what are you doing? Did you have a nice day?' What hurt the most was the difference in the tone of voice when the boys were sitting together taking the call and seeing the change in facial expression. It was painful for me to see and listen to. I couldn't even defend him. Children may not understand but they have feelings.

'Come here, give me a hug,' his dad used to say.

'No!' he would respond.

'Okay then, don't,' followed. How about questioning the reason why he said no?

Seeing my ex-husband showing favouritism was hard. I remember having to point out what he said or let him know that it was not nice nor the right way to speak to him. How about rephrasing it or changing the approach? He couldn't see it the way I saw it. What he did was right for him.

Looking back, people used to say one was a 'mummy's boy'. Of course, Mummy understood him. Mummy knew what he was going through. A child can learn from what is taught, learning from what you are told is different.

Through research, it came to me, that it could be because his parents spoke to him in the same way when he was young. His way of dealing with it was to prove them wrong. Well, it makes sense, but doesn't work with everyone. I also empathise with the fact that we often parent the way we were parented, despite everyone being an individual with different needs. Sometimes it's hard to adapt. I guess it's harder for males.

Simon Alexander Ong mentions in his book *Energize* about a research study by Carnegie Mellon University psychologists who found that supportive and encouraging couples were a core component in individual success. Brooke Feeney, lead author of the study, highlighted that, "significant others can help you thrive through embracing life opportunities or they hinder your ability to thrive by making it less likely that you'll pursue opportunities for growth."

As the boys got older, showing more affection for one boy was obvious; they noticed it too. Putting people down was what my ex-husband was good at. No wonder my son lacked confidence. He used to be afraid to do or say what he felt as he would be knocked down. I was left to deal with having to boost my son's confidence. I tried so many strategies, but only got temporary results. I remember always being the one to praise him for what he did well, let him make decisions, understand why he felt the way he did, be a bit more considerate and compromised, but it was no good just coming from me.

Over time, I knew it was not a healthy relationship nor

was it healthy for the boys to see their parents shouting at each other regularly.

I knew I needed help. My son needed it more. However, I didn't know where to start, especially because I couldn't stand seeing him having angry outbursts and was obviously unhappy. People around him would see him as being difficult, unhappy or just not wanting to join in. Nobody knew the reasons behind it, nobody knew what was going on behind closed doors. Many of my arguments with his dad stemmed from the way he spoke to and responded to our son.

It turned out that he bottled up everything his role model (dad) had said to him… of course, a boy will believe what his dad says. It knocked his confidence so much that the only way he could express his feelings was through anger… with a capital D – Danger!

It wasn't until I saw the transformation in a dear friend's daughter over time that I complimented on. Her words were, "It's that life coach she's been seeing." That was a light bulb moment for me… that's what I need for my son! After five coaching sessions when he was nine, he was able to change his mindset, and he was able to control his emotions and actions more confidently. The life coach managed to point out that his dad had something to do with his confidence. That's when I had to have that dreaded talk with my ex-husband. I reminded him of all the things he had said to our son and gave him examples of times when he had put him down. The response I got was, "Don't be silly, I didn't mean the things I said and, anyway, he should do better then. He's too young to remember anything." I was lost for words.

When my son returned from his next weekend with his dad, he told me, "Daddy said sorry for all the times he said all the bad things to me."

"Okay, how did it make you feel?" was all I could say.

"But Mummy, he's... five years too late," was the answer I got as he counted on his fingers. That confirmed it for me, that children really do remember and bottle up how people make them feel by what they say or do. Throughout my studies, I learnt that positive or negative experiences during the brain development of a five-to-seven year old can add up to shape a child's development and can have lifelong effects. Up until today, I imagine, my son subconsciously thinks he's 'stupid'. Obviously, he is not.

My son reminded me recently, "Remember I never used to believe in myself? I do now. I really have to put my mind to something to achieve it." He is no longer scared of failing because he knows that he can learn from failure. He knows what he wants and is able to solve problems on his own. I love how resilient he is. He doesn't care what anyone else thinks. He sure has an attitude for gratitude and is so happy knowing it's okay to express his feelings so people know exactly how he feels rather than bottling it up. What a headstrong young man he has become.

I know as a parent I cannot coach my own boys, but it definitely helps that I have a more positive mindset and know that it's okay to ask for help. Being proactive about helping children is brave and could be the best thing we can invest in them to last a lifetime. A bit like buying insurance to know that all will be okay as we have what we need to help and support our children when life throws curveballs at them. There is always a reason why we are the way we are. Knowing what it is and being aware of our emotions and experiences makes such a big difference… it's priceless.

Thinking back, when we first separated, my brother was more upset than me. "But you're going to be on your own… Do you know how sad and lonely that is?"

For me, it was more like, "Do you know how sad it is to be married and alone?"

I often speak to people and see similar behaviour in parents and their children. I'm so glad I was the proactive mum who sought professional help as I couldn't do it myself. I knew my marriage was unhealthy, but I didn't feel brave enough to suggest a separation as I thought it was normal for things to be the way they were, plus the questions: what am I going to do? Where am I going to go? (Who knows what life would have been like for all of us if we had stayed together.)

Fortunately, both my boys have developed into happy, grateful, respectful, independent, fine young men and are able to confidently deal with, express and control their emotions and actions. This has led me (and them) to be more confident in myself and as a mum after some self-development, mentors and life coaches along the way. I have worked on my mindset, got rid of limiting beliefs and am more focused in reaching my goals. We have a family brand where we share the same values. It is gratifying to see how resilient my boys were during the global pandemic to be now studying full-time and working part-time.

Thankfully, my circumstances have made me the person I am today. I love my own company, I love having the freedom to do what I want, when I want and how I want. My boys are approaching adulthood. I am ready to find happiness in love. I am more than ready to find my soulmate to share my life with.

After many years of doing what I love – working with children – I knew I could follow my passion to help and support children away from the school environment. I felt there was a need for me to empower children to be the best they can be. Having always loved the idea of a life coach as an adult, I found my purpose – to coach children. It is a newer concept, just not as recognised yet.

I certified as a kids' life coach in March 2019. I have been helping parents who struggle to boost their children's confidence. It's because of my own experiences that I chose boosting children's confidence as my niche. My passion in nurturing children's minds has come from my understanding of my own needs as a child. With many success stories of children I have coached, I have helped them navigate their emotions and prepared them for the challenges they will face growing up, providing them with a skill set to deal with life's ups and downs. Most importantly, they have a toolkit to last a lifetime.

While families may turn to a psychologist or therapist, kids' life coaching has proven to show and measure progress in the areas of the needs of each child.

My mission is to educate, motivate and inspire children to be the best they can be.

My vision is for children of the future to be confident leaders of their own life.

I love how I have become a lifelong learner. I never thought I'd go back to studying in my forties, let alone be reading more than I ever have.

Mental health is a topic of conversation with parents, carers and professionals that I speak to... Yes! Absolutely! Did you know, according to Mental Health Foundation (https://www.mentalhealth.org.uk/explore-mental-health/statistics/children-young-people-statistics):

> '10% of children and young people (aged 5-16) have a clinically diagnosable mental health problem, yet 70% of children and adolescents who experience mental health problems have not had appropriate interventions at a sufficiently early age.'

Scary, I know! Which is why I believe prevention is better than cure.

Anyone who can relate to my story, know that you are not alone, as much as it sometimes feels like you are. It's okay to reach out for help. You are not stuck, as much as you may think that you cannot move on without a partner or husband – think about what is healthier 'for the sake of the kids'... there is hope. Hold on to it!

★★★

I dedicate this book to my sons who have been on this journey with me – Kian for his resilience and helping me tell this story, Tate for being so understanding and always seeing the positives in every situation.

Candy's life changed when she discovered a children's life coach for her son. She worked on her own self-development and is today nurturing minds as a happy and successful international kids' life coach. She is a Brand Ambassador for The Kids Life Studio.

Candy is passionate about children's mental well-being and believes 'prevention is better than cure' and that it's okay to ask for help.

https://linktr.ee/candyfung

Listen to the audio version here:
https://bit.ly/INeededHelpSonNeededItMore

EVERYTHING HAPPENS
FOR A REASON

Jeannette Jones

"It never hurts to keep looking for sunshine."
> – *Eeyore*

I was asked if I wanted to write a chapter in this book. The title *Hold on to Hope* I thought was great as it gives people the opportunity to explain what hope means to them and how their lives have created different definitions. So, let's try and explain how hope lives with me.

I'm very much an "everything happens for a reason" type of person; accept what happens and how it happens and why it happens. So, I am a very practical person. I do try and be realistic.

I was born in 1970. By 2009, I was divorced and had two adorable girls. I had always hoped that I was not going to be another divorce statistic, but alas, no.

My youngest suffered horrendously with eczema. She must have been 90% covered. It was so painful that she did not have a bath until she was four, as even water stung. "They" suggested wet wrapping to me – I thought this barbaric, so I didn't. How could I have soaked bandages off every night when water stung? I had hoped I had made the right decision.

I made all her all-in-one pyjamas, as there was nothing on the market which catered for older children at this time. Any professional photos I had taken were always softened so her skin did not look as bad.

Every night, I hoped that she would sleep through – she did not. This did not actually happen until she was about four. I vowed that I would not have any more children as I would not be able to witness that pain and suffering again. As a parent, I took my responsibilities very seriously.

I always hoped that I'd made the right decision… where was the manual?

Being the adult, my decisions were also for my children – were they the right ones? Could I have made better ones?

Moving on. When I was thirty, I was rushing about around town, late, couldn't find the car in the car park, needed to be back for my children, and I noticed that one of my eyes was blurry. I just put it down to a blood pressure thing as I had been rushing about.

Well, I hoped it was.

I made an appointment with my GP, who then referred me to a consultant – so it wasn't what I had hoped for, then?

After an MRI, I was shown my scan – I was very impressed with it! I am sure I was not meant to have been! It was like someone had blobbed Tipex all about my brain. I was told each blob was scarring. The reason why my vision was blurry was that I had a scar on my optic nerve. When this nerve expanded, due to heat, the scar also expanded, so I was looking through my scar!

Oh, I had hoped not.

Multiple sclerosis it was then! I later found out that I ticked all the boxes for being a prime candidate – female, mid-twenties to mid-thirties and not living that close to the equator (Southampton, UK).

MS is where the body attacks the sheath, which is the covering of the nerves. As this can't be repaired, the body looks for other ways to make that action happen, which is why fatigue plays a massive role – everything takes more effort.

Oh.

My doctor signed me off work for three months, which I thought was unnecessary.

I hoped it was unnecessary.

I needed to get my head around the fact that I now had an incurable degenerative condition that "they" do not know how you get. It does take a lot of getting your head around. I was actually really pleased about the fact that I had three months off from work. I was introduced to Lisa Black, who was going to be my MS nurse. She was amazing – fun, bubbly and optimistic. Everything I needed.

I hoped that she was going to help me through this.

She did.

I did not tell my parents about it for nearly three years. I knew that my dad would blame himself because his mum had multiple sclerosis.

I hoped that he wouldn't, but he did.

He went to the doctor, he blamed himself, and he found out about it. It is not hereditary, but there is "tendency to it".

There are three types of MS: relapsing and remitting – you have a temporary dip and get back to where you were (nearly); secondary progressive – you go downhill slowly; and primary progressive – you go downhill quickly.

I hoped that I didn't have primary progressive.

Phew, only (!) secondary progressive.

Lisa invited me along to a couple of things. One was a monthly "ladies that lunch" and the other was the local MS treatment centre. I declined both. I didn't want to see what I could be! To this day, I have not looked up MS on the internet. I can manage my life as it is right now, I cannot take on other people's.

After about a year, I plucked up the courage to visit the lunch. It was going to be small, ladies only. I was petrified. They were all relatively young, friendly and welcoming.

I hoped that I was not going to need a wheelchair or need walking aids, like all the other ladies in the meeting.

I currently have a stick (no wheelchair).

I've always seen my life as a moving normal! I thank my lucky stars every day that I can still do as much as I can do now. When I get a new symptom, that is going to be my new "normal", as it will not be going away. My normal symptoms currently include balance issues, I can't look up without getting dizzy, can't walk very far, fatigue and I have neuropathic pain, which is currently primarily down my right side.

I hope that this does not start affecting my left side.

There is nothing I can do, it will go where it wants to.

After a few months of "lunching", I agreed to meet Lisa at the local MS treatment centre. It was only five or six miles away from home.

It is a charity, with a manager plus one, and the rest is staffed by volunteers. I was really nervous and scared to see what I may become, what may happen. It was a very airy, fresh open building. The main reception area was the "café". I was made very welcome, and everyone just went about and did what "healthy" people did! Chatted, drank coffee, read, etc. Some were in wheelchairs, some with sticks, some had carers, some needed to drink with a straw, some needed a hoist to be moved about, but it seemed a very positive environment.

Selfishly (?) I hoped I wasn't going to get as bad as some of those people I saw.

But what it did make me realise was that whatever you were like on the outside, it's what is on the inside that matters. And if you can see past the physical, you actually could see the person inside. These people seemed happy, laughter was heard, they took the mickey out of either themselves or each other and didn't take themselves too seriously. They all had "normal lives" before MS.

I hoped I could be like that.

I am glad that I took time before I went there, as I could see that if I wasn't in the right head space, it could have gone the other way and I wouldn't have been able to cope.

I ended up becoming a fundraiser, and I had some great

friends who supported whatever I did! These included fundraisers at the centre: Mother's Day pamper weekends, fashion shows, afternoon tea, Christmas gift fayres, sponsored days at the races, etc. I raised over £20,000 and, I suppose more importantly, awareness for the centre and other people like me.

I hope I made people aware that if you have a disability there are still lots of things you can do!

I have always said that as long as I know that somebody is doing something I will always have hope. If there are still scientists, if there are still nurses, doctors, surgeons, anybody still trying to find out how, why, which and when, I still have hope. It's always hopeful when you know specialists of different neurological conditions are starting to work together to try and find a cure for this and other neurological conditions.

With hope and my practicality, I have realised that life is far too short, there's no time to be grumpy, or to worry about things which don't matter. I know that this has helped me immensely with my journey. It makes me quite sad, really, to wonder why I had to have something so life-changing happen before I actually realised what is important and what isn't.

I have hope.

This was easily shown when my granddaughter, who was only two at the time, visited with my daughter. She was playing with a mosaic bowl on my coffee table. It was something that I'd brought back from Barcelona. Miya was playing with it. She dropped it and it broke. My daughter was so upset. She suggested that I get it glued back together. I told her to throw it away, it was just a "thing", and it was not important. What was important was that Miya had not hurt herself. The bowl was incidental. Why did I have to be diagnosed with a critical condition before I knew what was important?

I hope that I am making sure my children are aware of priorities.

As previously mentioned, two out of three people who get MS are female, which may be why my brother hasn't got it. And my mum hasn't, but it wasn't on her side, it was from my dad's. I have two daughters and my granddaughter. I hope and I pray that they don't get it. But there is nothing I can do. I cannot change what is going to happen with them. It's like with any condition, any disease, any anything. Nobody knows if you're going to get cancer or have a heart attack or a blood clot or a stroke, or get run over by a bus, there is nothing you can do. But you can try to improve your lifestyle. You can change little things like diet and exercise.

I hope that my girls don't get MS.

The problem is, though, we don't know how, why, when, if…

I just hope with every part of me that they stay healthy.

The only thing that they do know is that the closer to the equator you are, the more likely you are not to get it. So, unless we can all emigrate to the South of France, I don't really know what else we can do.

I currently have MS down my right side. It's in my

right leg and my right arm. I can still walk; I don't need a wheelchair. I do have to use a stick. I've got numb bits and neuropathic pain and I fall over everything or nothing! I often forget a word or sentence. Names, just forget it – everyone is "dear" or "lovely" or "chuck". It is as I have said before, a moving normal. Every day is different, different things happen. I wake up every morning and give thanks for everything that I can still do.

I always hope that today is going to be as good as yesterday.

If yesterday was bad, I hope that today will be better, or different, at least.

I am a very practical person, sometimes I think too much. I am unable to give blood, or donate parts of my body after death, as it is not known how you can get MS. So, I have already put my name down on the MS tissue bank. This allows stem tissue collection for future investigation.

I hope that my death brings the understanding of this condition nearer to its cure. I do not want my life to have been for no reason.

I have never given up on thinking positively – you may think of it as being hopeful. I appreciate waking up every day and nothing is taken for granted – it can be taken away in an instant.

Live in hope.

★★★

I would like to dedicate my chapter to my girls – Charlotte, Harriet and Miya – please never give up hope.

Jeannette is a grandma on a mission! Her beautiful granddaughter Miya came along a bit earlier than she expected, making her a grandma at forty-five! Jeannette was, internally, mortified, but of course also knew how blessed she was. Miya's arrival got Jeannette thinking about the state of things in the world. It's the topic on everyone's lips but no one seems to know what to do to prevent the deterioration of our environment. It seems like an overwhelming task to 'save the world'! What animals would be around for Miya to see when she got older? Whether it be a hedgehog or a turtle, this made Jeannette realise that something had to be done. And not just for her granddaughter but for everyone's grandchildren.

After discovering Wikaniko, she quickly realised that we don't have to take on this huge task all by ourselves. If each one of us were to do a few little things each day that barely even cause an inconvenience, and, in fact, often benefit us and save us money, then we can all do this together.

You don't have to single-handedly save the world, just make a few ripples. Jeannette hopes that by letting you know about the products available here, it will give you the power to choose. And by choosing to make little changes in your daily buying habits, then you can have that incredible feeling of making a difference.

https://linktr.ee/anygreenwilldo

Listen to the audio version here:
https://bit.ly/EverythingHappensforaReason

LIVING WITH AND LEAVING
AN ADDICT

Alison Harding

*"You don't have to see the whole staircase to
take the first step."*
– Martin Luther King

Have you ever been in a situation where, for whatever
reason, you just cannot make sense of what's going on, how
you got there, or the person you have become? For me,
that situation was the ending of my marriage. Here I was,
standing outside a storage trailer, looking at twenty boxes
of various shapes and sizes that accounted for the leftovers
of my twenty-year marriage. I was exhausted – emotionally,
physically and mentally. To see my whole life boxed up in
a storage container in the middle of an industrial estate in
a small town in Scotland after a very long drive was utterly
heart-wrenching.

As the tears flowed down my face, I just thought to
myself, 'why?' Why did I devote a major chunk of my life,
my heart and my soul to this person who had stripped me
bare of every individual characteristic that identified me?
This person who had caused me so much pain and anguish

for years – so why did I not leave sooner?

To the outside world, I was in a good marriage. My husband worked hard to provide for us a beautiful home, allowing us to play out the dream of living in the sun. I used to describe my marriage as blissful, peaceful, with the perfect balance of my having 'me' time when he was away working and then our quality time as a family with our two fur babies. Family and friends would come to us for holidays and marvel at the beautiful and happy life we had, or that they believed we had. However, it was only after moving to that beautiful island that my eyes were opened and my heart truly broken. Just like an episode of the TV show of the same name, the dream was short and sweet.

Growing up, I loved Disney movies – in fact, I still do – and I always fantasised about being the lead character with the knight in shining armour sweeping me off my feet, taking me away from the pain and suffering that existed within my childhood and living happily ever after. The adult version of me, of course, knew that in reality any marriage was not like the movies. It was no fairy tale, but more a working partnership that involves compromise. The problem with that is, when you marry someone who has hidden addictions, you end up being the one doing all the compromising. Well, I certainly did.

In my working life, I had a vast experience of dealing with and recognising those who had addictions or addictive personalities. I had worked with a number of clients who suffered from addictions and trauma. I could help someone recognise their issues and provide them with the skills and knowledge to empower themselves to have enriching lives whilst in recovery. However, when it came to myself and my home environment, for whatever reason, those traits, triggers and 'aha' moments were so subtle and unrecognisable to me that I just seemed blinded to it. They were extremely well hidden – not only from me but from those around me – and I now acknowledge I also had a part to play in that illusion being portrayed to the outside world, including to immediate family and friends. This is where shame took over and I participated in the illusion in order to protect myself and those around me from the truth. My husband was an alcoholic. It was only many years later that I found out a number of friends had recognised what was going on but didn't want to say anything through fear of hurting my feelings, or embarrassing me, even though my husband managed to do that on a daily basis, especially in the later years.

My husband worked in an industry that took him across the world. His working environments, whether it be in the middle of the sea or in a foreign country, meant that when he came home his main method of relaxation was alcohol. Drinking to excess in a very short period of time was explained away by myself on many occasions. I would explain to people that because he worked away, in order to provide a comfortable living and lifestyle for us, his excesses were a natural part of his work and home life balance. Ha! Who on earth was I kidding? The words 'excesses' and 'natural' should not be in the same sentence. But I just continued making up excuses for him.

I withdrew from invites for dinner out with other couples and larger groups of friends because I could not sit there whilst he got excessively drunk and then worry about the words that would come out of his mouth. At times, he was not a pleasant drunk. On other occasions, he was just silent and not engaging in conversation, just wanting to go to the bar, whilst I was constantly watching him out of the corner of my eye to make sure he did not say anything or do anything to upset someone. I was always in a heightened state of alert.

But, at the time, I really did believe that I could manage his addiction and cope with the changing personalities and behaviours of the person I was once in love with. You see, I believed in my marriage vows; for better or worse, for richer or poorer, in sickness and in health. How could I complain about his behaviour when he was providing me the ability to have this beautiful home in the sun? It was everyone's dream, wasn't it? How dare I question the man and his behaviour when he was working so hard to provide a roof over my head. When you have been homeless – as I had been in my younger years – that ideal of a roof over your head is paramount to your basic safety needs. As time went on, his addictions slowly started to chip away at me. So why did I stay? I stayed because I loved him. It's as simple as that. He was my knight in shining armour and had promised to love me the way I deserved after a traumatic childhood. I truly believed that with enough support he would begin to realise what was at stake and what he could lose.

In his mind, he didn't recognise the addiction, denying for years that he had a problem. How could he have a problem? He was *numero uno* as far as he was concerned, and he liked to ensure everyone knew it. Especially me. His internal battle was not alcohol but that need to prove himself as being the best in whichever field he was competing. This was especially true in relation to his professional environment. To be number one and have the associated status that came along with it was essential to his ego and drive. I can remember once being in a social situation with him and some of his work colleagues, and whilst he was talking to a newly qualified person in the same field as him, he was telling them that no matter how good they were, their certification number would always be higher than his. The colleague appeared confused or annoyed – or both, more likely – but he was inferring to his colleague that he was better because he did it first. This was where he got his validation from. The alcohol was an ego boost, and he became narcissistic in his demeanour, believing he was 'top dog'. The colleague just looked at me with pity in his eyes. Yet I felt the need to apologise. Why was I apologising for his behaviour? I felt I was being judged by everyone in the room at this point and had to leave. I turned down any further invites that involved my husband. It was safer that way.

With more drinking came more consequences. This eventually became untenable as the addiction took hold. What was it that was at the bottom of the bottle that made him continue to seek it out? I know that was not the way to think, but it was how I felt. I allowed his behaviour and choices to become my life and choices. Jobs that were initially easy to obtain due to his reputation were also becoming jobs very easy to lose due to his addiction and the impact this was having on his ability to function. Meanwhile, I was back in our 'idyllic home', taking care of everything, trying to cope with messed up finances, but not being allowed to address them. I was always reminded it was his money, he earned it, so he would decide how it got used when it came to big bills – and there were many. Meanwhile, I continued telling the family all was well, in order for them not to get stressed and worry about him.

As the years passed, more jobs came and went, each one lost through his alcohol addiction. Why could I not just leave? Admitting I had failed at something was extremely hard for me and that was exactly what I thought. That I was the one who had failed because, no matter what I did to try and ensure he was safe in whichever country he was in, it was never enough. Turning up at airports to collect him only for him to not come through those arrival doors. Either because he had passed out in the toilets after downing whatever he had purchased in the duty lounge or because he was so drunk that he was refused travel and could not be sober enough to let me know. The distress and anxiety I felt every time I walked away from airports not knowing where he was or what had happened was crippling me.

And still I pretended. It was only when I had to report him missing in different countries that I realised things were getting out of control, his addiction was getting out of control, and I could do nothing about it. I was stubborn, though, and I was determined that I would not be defeated. I started to open up to the family and let them know what was going on. But they struggled to understand or accept that he had an issue. How could he have an issue when he had these amazing jobs across the world? My guilt and shame in letting them know was exacerbated by their responses, so again I withdrew and covered for him.

It was always there. I just wanted him to see that I loved him. Why was that not good enough? He asked me to marry him all those years ago. Where was the person I fell in love with? It was a significant point when I realised that I no longer respected the person in front of me. When he realised this, the manipulation and emotional blackmail increased significantly. As I tried to support him through withdrawal for the fifth time, he would threaten to kill himself with a bread knife or anything else that was at hand. And, in the same breath, would tell me that he didn't want children (we had struggled for years to have children – my biggest dream was to become a mum) and had lied to me throughout our marriage in order to keep me as the constant success in his life. This was another part of the addiction that no one knew about. Even though I struggle to talk about it, I did recognise the behaviour of someone who hates themselves so much that they could not accept their true self. So, I watched helplessly as our lives imploded around us as every door was slammed in his face. He spiralled into a very dark place.

We had lost everything. Our home, our belongings, that whole part of our lives was finished. We had to move back in with his parents. By this point, I was a shell of my former self. I had withdrawn from friends, family, from everything that gave me the slightest bit of joy. My only constant was my fur babies. Their unconditional love was my saving grace and reason for getting up each day. I was also lucky enough to have some persistent friends who were there for me through thick and thin. It was difficult for them to watch me go through this pain, but they just let me know they were there for me and that was enough. I realised I did not need to feel so alone because I wasn't. I was lonely in my marriage but not alone in my life. It took me quite a long time to truly believe that. I am so grateful for that power of unconditional love because it saved me. It also helped me understand the need for self-love and self-care. The best self-care was for me to take the courageous step and leave. This was the hardest thing I had ever had to do in my life because by leaving I still felt I had failed. My marriage had failed. I had failed as a wife.

But I also began to realise there is no shame in failure. Failure provides us lessons to learn and that is where the successes arise from. In order to leave, I still felt I had to make sure he had access to all the support he needed. And this is what I did. I supported him in recovery services, medical services and support services. He chose to manipulate those situations and not change his behaviours, meaning his family began to realise the extent of his addictions. I had opened their eyes to it, so I knew he would have them and no longer needed me to look after him. Our second fur baby was no longer with us by this time and my final tie to my old life had come to an end. I needed to look after myself. And so, I also sought support for myself. Was that selfish of me? Yes, it was, but sometimes being selfish means we can truly invest in ourselves. That support allowed me the space to breathe and the opportunity to reframe many situations in my life, where rather than continue to punish myself for my failings, I actually did a damn good job of surviving and managing effectively for as long as I did. I also recognise that there were many happy occasions during my marriage, and I have some wonderful memories, for which I am thankful.

I've shared my story so that it can demonstrate that leaving an addict is nothing to be ashamed of. It is nothing to feel guilty about because I realised I am not responsible for someone else's choices. I cannot be their saviour. No matter how much you love someone, they have to love themselves first. Sadly, my husband didn't. I was not failing in my marriage, I was finally rejecting the negative impact my marriage was having on me. I do believe rejection is protection and redirection. So, as I stood outside that container filled with my belongings, tears rolling down my face, the answer to my question – why did I not leave sooner was this – was that I had many lessons to learn in order to be redirected onto this new part of my journey. For all the pain and anguish, I am also relieved, as I am now in a much happier place. I have purpose, a passion for life and I am excited for my future. I took time to heal – I will always be healing. I have forgiven myself, forgiven him and I have let go. I now know anything is possible when you truly invest in yourself.

★★★

I would like to dedicate this chapter to all of those friends who helped me stand in my truth – I call them my earth angels. To Universal Source for the gift of energy, love and light. Namaste.

Alison is a Lightworker and Energist, using the modality of EMO (Energy in Motion) to support others in their journey of self-discovery. Alison is currently awaiting completion of her Level 2 practitioner accreditation in EFT (Emotional Freedom Technique).

Alison was aware of the power of energy from a very early age and developed her skills and knowledge to enable her to help people shine their light from within.

Throughout her life, Alison has faced a number of adversities and challenges, which have made her the person she is today. Alison believes she is always learning and healing, and aims to support as many people as she can through her use of energy work to feel uplifted, enlightened and at peace inside themselves, both on a spiritual and physical level, creating their own toolkits to deal with issues or challenges they may face in order to become the best version of themselves.

https://linktr.ee/alba_h

Listen to the audio version here:
https://bit.ly/Livingwithandleavinganaddict

LIVING WITH IMPOSTER SYNDROME

Charlotte Lewington

> *"It is our responsibility to create, educate, integrate and
> upgrade ourselves to be the best version of ourselves.
> To be inspiring role models and motivators for our own
> children is our own moral obligation as much as our
> initial right."*
>
> *– Boryana Hristova*

Social media has taken the world by storm over the last
decade. So many people are now taking to different
social media platforms in order to show the best version
of themselves, as well as encouraging people to live their
dream life by being able to work from a phone or laptop
anywhere in the world. Whilst this all sounds amazing and
what most people would love to do, the reality is sometimes
completely the opposite. The reason why I mention social
media is because the number of people with mental health
difficulties is at an all-time high. There are so many people
who are experiencing feelings of not being enough as they
are, constantly comparing themselves to other people and
having unrealistic expectations.

So many of my clients tell me that they feel they have to

do or be something they are not in order to be successful. If there is one thing that I want to make you aware of it's that social media makes you think, "Maybe I should be somewhere else doing something else with someone else." If you always think your happiness is somewhere else, it will never be where you are.

Everybody wants to have a nice home, car, more money and be successful, but everyone's version of success is different. When it comes to success, there is no such thing as becoming an overnight sensation or being able to earn six figures in a short space of time. For many, the truth is that they have been working for years behind the scenes in order to get to that point. One of my main values is that I believe in being authentic and transparent. I am not going to write this chapter and tell you that running a business or designing a life you love is easy.

Within my courses, I teach people about the importance of self-awareness and setting boundaries so that they start to believe in themselves and not settle for anything less than the best for themselves. The reason I teach this within my course is because when I started to do this for myself, my life changed for the better. All my life, I have struggled with feeling confident in my abilities. I struggled to find my voice and speak up and say what I felt when I really wanted to. I stayed quiet for years, thinking that I didn't have anything important to say. It was only when I started looking really deep at how other people's opinions had dented my confidence that I learnt how I could change my perception and view on life.

I write this chapter to encourage people to know that they are enough just as they are and that we are not always perfect and that is okay. As long as we learn to embrace our flaws, we can learn to love ourselves unconditionally.

Growing up, my life hasn't always been easy, but both my parents were amazing and always tried to give me the best opportunities possible. I always had two holidays, two Christmases and my parents always made sure that I was cared and provided for. However, the situations life presented have been challenging. People often say that life is a constant series of lessons. I believe that learning the lessons are the key to being able to live a happy, fulfilling, meaningful life. Yet many people go through life without ever asking what they have learned each day.

Being mindful of learning daily lessons enables us to be open to change and grow. It also enables us to be able to cope with the situations that we are going through. Somehow, life has a way of teaching us lessons that we would not normally learn otherwise. Some of life's lessons I would rather not have learnt and that is exactly what makes life such an excellent teacher. If life was predictable and always in control, how would we learn?

Through the experiences I have faced, I believe that we have two options in life: we can either sit down and cry about things or we get up and try to learn the lesson that is being shown to us. There are many times I look back and believe that my life could have turned out a lot differently if I hadn't made the good choices and decisions that I have. I also believe that my parents' influence also guided me in the right direction. No matter how much I argued and fought against them, I later learnt that they were right and only wanted the best for me at the time.

Throughout my life experiences, I have been able to learn that things do not always go as planned, despite our best intentions, but if we can learn and grow from what life teaches us, it makes it a little bit easier to manage. During the hard times, I wasn't always able to see the lesson being shown to me straight away but, in time, I was able to figure it out. As a teenager, you think you know it all. I am very stubborn in nature and always wanted to figure things out on my own. I consider it to be true that you will keep getting the same lessons until you are able to change what you are doing and figure out the lesson you are meant to learn. It is the same with people. I believe that people will come into your life when they are meant to. There are many people you will encounter, and each of them can teach you a valuable lesson if you look for the lesson being taught. Some people will come into your life for a reason, a season or a lifetime. Part of my journey has involved being able to deal with a lot of heartache and pain, but I have used that pain as my superpower. The heartache that you go through can strengthen you or destroy you. You have a choice.

Crying is our emotional connection with the world. The simple act is often seen as a weakness when it is actually the strength in us. It is okay to cry about things, as it is a natural reaction of our body and one that promotes a healthier mind. There is a great quote that says, "Don't forget that you are human." It is okay to have a meltdown, just don't unpack and stay there. Cry it out and then refocus on where you are headed. It is important to cry about hard things, but it is also important to use them to drive you and not paralyse you. There were many times that I just wanted to give up. However, the little fighter inside me knew better than that. Giving up was never an option. There is always something better coming, even when it feels like you are facing rock bottom. Sometimes you need to know what rock bottom feels like in order to lift yourself up from it. It is in the darkest moments that you must focus on seeing the light. Anyone can be happy, positive and grateful when everything is going well, but when nothing is going well that is when we truly need to focus our minds and dig deep.

It is a well-known fact that the first 1001 days – including pregnancy and the first two years – of a child's life are a significant and influential phase in development. Within this stage, the foundations can be laid for every child's future health, well-being, learning and earnings potential. It sets the groundwork for children being able to develop their emotional well-being, resilience and adaptability; the competencies they need to thrive. I believe it is a fundamental stage that all parents, carers and childcare professionals need to know about.

During this period in my life, by the age of three, my brother was diagnosed with a terminal illness and unfortunately passed away by the time I was six years old. The reason I tell you about this moment is because I believe it is pivotal in being able to understand the person I am today and why I have struggled with confidence issues and imposter syndrome for so many years of my life. Someone once asked me why I decided to work with children and I always thought it was because I had a passion for working with them. I thought they were so young but yet were able to learn and know so much, but maybe deep down there was the subconscious belief that I wanted to protect children, to help them overcome the emotions that I felt as a child and guide them through those difficult times.

As part of my personal development journey and academic studies, I have been able to understand how a child who has experienced adverse childhood experiences (ACES) may think or feel. One of the symptoms that I believe I learnt as a coping mechanism was the need to always be busy doing something. I began to realise that I was always on high alert, thinking that I was going to get into trouble if I was found to be sitting down and not doing something. There are some great conversations I have had with people who ask me what I do for work and, when I reel off everything that I have going on, they are amazed by how I fit it all in.

Hypervigilance is a common fight or flight effect that people who have experienced trauma can display. A person or child who is hypervigilant feels constantly on edge and fearful. Sometimes I would experience a sense of dread like I was under threat, despite the fact there was no present danger. People in authority roles intimidated me and I always used to feel inferior to them. It was only when I started to work in the emergency department and had to have conversations with consultants and operational leaders that I started to face this fear and began to see people in authority as normal everyday people, despite the title or position of power that they had. It was during these times that I began to realise how much I had achieved and what I was capable of. I started to take the right action to help me to change my life and design the life I wanted to live, without worrying about pleasing other people.

If you had asked me five years ago where I saw my life going, I would never have believed that I would become an entrepreneur with my own business. It was only when I joined a network marketing company that I was able to open my eyes to a different way of living life. Network marketing is not just about the selling. The opportunity enabled me to figure out what personal development was and led me on a journey of self-awareness and self-discovery. It made me question who Charlotte was: what did I enjoy doing, what was my favourite colour, what excited me, what do I stand for? I asked myself if I was happy and, if I wasn't, why was that? I began to really dig deep and go within. It is during this time that I really began to understand how my childhood had had an impact on me more than I'd realised.

Throughout my childhood, I started to believe from other people's comments and behaviour that I wasn't very likeable. I thought that I irritated people and that I was stupid. For years, I was a people pleaser who went along with what I thought other people wanted to hear instead of finding my own voice. We spend so much of our lives trying to fit in, to be liked, to be good enough, that we forget to be our true selves. We believe the things we do because of how we are conditioned in childhood. For years, I tried to change who I was in order to be liked and to fit it. It wasn't until my own self-development journey that I found out who I was and what it really means to be unapologetic for who I am.

I believe that I have suffered from imposter syndrome. Imposter syndrome can be defined as the persistent inability to believe that one's success is deserved or has been legitimately achieved as a result of one's own efforts or skills. In order to understand the context and for transparency, I would like to explain that I am qualified with a level three cache diploma in childcare and education, a bachelor of science degree in psychology, I am an international accredited coach, I have a corporate training and executive coaching diploma, and I am currently studying towards a master's in children and young people. My courses and business have been accredited by the CPD organisation. I have sixteen years' experience of working with children and young people and have experience of working in the NHS at an operational level. I am a two times best-selling co-author. I have trained in rapid transformation therapy. But, despite all these credentials, it is only within the last few years that I have truly believed that I have done enough training and I am now able to be considered an expert in my field.

People who struggle with imposter syndrome believe that they are undeserving of their achievements and the high esteem in which they are, in fact, generally held.

I believed that people didn't consider me as competent or intelligent. I remember taking part in my first radio appearance after my first book collaboration and, whilst talking about my story, I was worried that people would find me out and think I didn't know what I was talking about. I couldn't help but think people would think of me as a fraud. Looking back, I know this is all to do with the experiences I faced in school, and it is only because of my training that I now have the toolkit to be able to rewrite the meaning I had given that experience in order to overcome this fear.

Dealing with imposter syndrome is not easy; the constant self-doubting, over-analysing and constantly worrying about what other people think about you is tiring. It has not been easy, but I have learnt ways to be able to deal with the voices and to quieten them down so that I am not always doubting myself and my capabilities. One exercise I found really helpful was to write down all of my skills and abilities onto a piece a paper, as well as writing down all the things that I have achieved within my life. Once you start to read what you have written, it can be really surprising how much you have achieved. It can be too easy to keep going onto the next thing without taking the time to appreciate or acknowledge all the successes that we have achieved.

Although I have been through a lot and have days where I stay in my head a bit longer than I should do, I am really proud of everything that I have achieved. I am proud that I kept on going even on the days when I felt like giving up. It is through the life experience I have that

I am now able to help other people. Within my business, I am able to offer courses, workshops and retreats to both parents and childcare professionals. Throughout my sixteen years' experience working with children and young people in various different settings, I am now able to deliver high quality standards of childcare as well as teach other providers how to achieve the same. People are often worried when OFSTED are due to inspect their settings, but I always say if you are doing what you are supposed to be doing on a daily basis and know the policies and procedures, it is not as daunting as you think. It is my aim to be able to help other early years providers and schools to be able to offer high quality of standards within settings. Children are so innocent and vulnerable and look up to us as adults to be able to provide the right opportunities for them to be able to not just survive but thrive in life. For many children, the most important role models are the parents and caregivers. A role model is a person who serves as an example by influencing others. Children look up to a variety of role models to help how they behave in school, with relationships or when making difficult decisions. In today's society, children are turning to social media and the appearance of celebrities as people they look up to. It is so important for them to choose positive role models in order to achieve possible outcomes for themselves. It is my mission to be one of those positive role models because when I tell people what I do so many people say to me 'I wish I had someone like you when I was a child'.

***

I dedicate this book to anyone who has ever struggled to feel like they are seen, heard and validated. Everything comes down to our perception, the way we perceive ourselves and allow others to treat us. I provide you with my chapter to remind you and give you permission that you can be whatever you choose to believe and decide the person you were destined to be. I invite you to ask yourself who would you be if no one told you who you were?

Charlotte is a best-selling author, educator and consultant helping children and young people to find their voice, be seen and to feel validated. There is nothing she is more passionate about than making sure children know that they are loved and love themselves from the inside out. During her own childhood, Charlotte faced many struggles that only made her stronger. Through these experiences, she learnt that you can either sit down and cry about things or you get up and you move on, learning the lesson being shown to you.

After sixteen years' experience within different health and childcare settings, Charlotte gained a degree in psychology and is currently working towards a master's in children and young people.

Whilst working for the NHS, Charlotte realised just how precious life can be and that life can be cut short at any moment. So, she decided to follow her passion and her love for children and young people to set up her own business, Mente Hermosa Academy ('Beautiful Mind –

Beautiful You' in Spanish).

Charlotte has created her own CPD interactive training sessions that provide parents and childcare professionals with information on the current issues affecting children and young people, especially in regard to social media, body image and confidence issues.

Charlotte spends most of her time delivering training to nurseries, schools and organisations, offering workshops and retreats relating to emotional well-being.

Her mission is to provide support in order to bridge the gap with the mental health crisis that we are currently experiencing.

In between all this, you will often find Charlotte travelling the world and making the most out of life.

https://linktr.ee/mentehermosaacademy

Listen to the audio version here:
https://bit.ly/LivingwithImposterSyndrome

MY JOURNEY OF SELF-DISCOVERY

Sam Rawlings

"I have endured. I have been broken. I have known hardship. I have lost myself. But here I stand, still moving forward, growing stronger each day!"

– Unknown

Sunday afternoon, the sun is shining, a sense of peace and calmness and I'm enjoying doing nothing.

This is my journey of my trials and tribulations to becoming a children's creative counsellor.

Self-doubt is something I've struggled with for a long time. I found it hard to believe in myself, to trust in my instincts, how it had an impact on my self-worth, confidence, self-belief and who I'd become. Now feels the right time to share my story, to help others who might be struggling with their own mental health.

It's not been an easy journey. I've faced a real roller coaster of emotions and challenges to say the least, but I'm so proud of my achievements. I'm so proud of myself, my confidence has increased, and I've grown both personally and professionally. I'm definitely in a good place now, something I never thought achievable. I've got two amazing daughters who have supported me throughout these challenges. We've always been there for each other, but certain things I have to do on my own and this is one of them.

This is my story, which may be difficult to hear. It could help you feel empowered, but most of all it's to show you that you're not alone. There is always help out there no matter how dark things may seem.

I didn't find it easy throughout my childhood. I never felt listened to. My parents married young, my dad was self-employed and my mum stayed at home. They found it hard bringing up young children and when my brother and I were still quite young, they separated. We moved from a lovely home to a two-storey flat in a different location, but I soon made friends locally. Those were the good times as I think about them. I remember playing in the street and I became really good at hide and seek, skipping and ball games. We visited our grandparents and extended family quite often; weekends were family times. We had fun times together. My brother liked to play pranks, I remember when he shook a bottle of ketchup all over the kitchen ceiling and said it was blood, something I still laugh about now.

I'm the oldest of four, so I had extra responsibility; my job was to help with my siblings. When anything went wrong, I was always to blame. This knocked my confidence and self-esteem greatly and I became quiet and withdrawn.

I went through my own tough times, I was often

bullied in school, and from the age of five I wore glasses and patches for a squint which made it worse. I had a small group of friends. We moved areas on more than one occasion, and I always lost my friends and found it difficult to make new ones. Also, being born in September meant I was the eldest in the school year and so there were higher expectations to do well in my education.

I loved singing and joined my school choir. Thinking back now, singing helped me more than I realised. I was now quiet, shy and spent the majority of time on my own. I didn't feel I could turn to my family for support; they were going through their own challenges. I was isolated, lonely and didn't fit in anywhere.

Then things really took a turn for the worse.

I find it difficult to write this part, even after all these years. It still leaves a tightness in my throat. If someone would have told me then what I know now, it would have made a huge difference to my life. I suffered what no child should have to go through, and I still can't write the name for it. I surprised myself getting this far into my chapter and I am continually healing from my past trauma.

It was when I was about seven that things started to change. Mum had a new relationship, and initially everything seemed good. Then we moved and again I lost my friends and had to start a new school. This time it felt harder; something had changed. I had younger sisters and stepsisters of a similar age and still got the blame when things went wrong. I was unhappy and struggled in school. Luckily, there was a local guiding unit that I was able to join; it felt like I'd do anything to avoid being at home. Time seemed to stand still and I felt like a robot. I'd just nod; agree; 'Children were seen and not heard'. So, I learnt to stay quiet and to stay out of trouble. I was scared and frightened. I'd tried to speak to people in school, but again I wasn't listened to or believed, so I accepted everything that happened to me, even though deep down I knew it was wrong.

The trauma continued, but no one knew. I started to live a life of lies to protect myself. I just wanted to feel accepted, noticed and cared for.

In my early twenties, with two young children, I started my career. I trained as a nursery nurse and worked in various childcare settings. I was happy, settled and soon married. Unfortunately, it didn't work out, and in 2011 we separated.

Little did I know I would still feel triggered from my childhood trauma in my forties. A big empty space appeared in my life and home. My daughters had moved out and started their own lives. I struggled to believe in myself. I would continually think, 'I'm not good enough, or 'I don't deserve to be happy and reach my dreams.' I was in and out of therapy; some of them I found helpful, whilst others not. I was bullied and manipulated in my career, and had a lack of strength and assertiveness to protect and stand up for myself. It reached a point where I didn't want to get up, or get dressed. I struggled to leave the house and even tried on several occasions to take too many painkillers. However, at the back of my mind were my daughters and I knew I couldn't leave them alone. Something had to change…

My GP referred me to trauma group therapy and diagnosed me with F1 anxiety and depression. I was in denial for the first twelve weeks, and didn't fit in. I held a full-time job, owned a car and home. There was nothing wrong with me. I really had to dig deep to start the healing process. After twenty-three weeks, I'd grown, developed my confidence and walked out of the therapy door with my head held high. I'd gained new friendships and a whole load of tools to help me during struggles and challenging situations. I was aware I hadn't completely healed and there would always be something I may find triggering. But it was time to process everything I took away to continue to live my life fully.

One of the therapists told me during a conversation that I would make a good therapist and should write a book; I didn't believe her. I just laughed and shrugged it off. However, here I am, ten years later, writing my first chapter.

I'd also heard whilst working in the nursery that one in five children experience mental health issues from under five. I had noticed children and families with concerns and I wanted to make a difference, even if it was for one child. I wanted to help turn a negative situation into something positive.

Several years later, the start of my journey in counselling began with an introductory course initially to check I'd made the right decision. I soon realised how much I understood from first-hand experiences. In 2017, my life changed when I qualified as a person-centred counsellor. Of course, the training brought new challenges. A huge part of this was self-awareness and personal therapy. Imposter syndrome constantly reminding me of not being good enough. Eventually though, with the support from my fellow students and tutors, I believed in myself.

As an empath, I've always been really caring. I always put other people first, so I guess it was natural to develop my understanding.

I wasn't ready to go into private practice, so thought it would be good to gain experience with young people. All my previous jobs had been with children under five and primary school.

It felt like a new beginning, a new page in my book, with excitement and eagerness. I worked in children's residential homes to gain experience with teens with poor mental health. A challenging time and on reflection I see how I was triggered from my own traumatic experiences and how I did or didn't deal with them… I gained so much knowledge, especially around brain development from trauma and, in 2020, I felt ready to start my own practice. I wanted to move away from constant tiredness, aches and pains from overworking and the stresses attached to such an emotionally challenging job.

I'd hit a real low and knew now was the time for a big change. My mental health wasn't good, and I had physical ailments. I couldn't sleep, had a poor diet and I'd stopped caring for myself. I'd get up, go to work, arrive home the following day and go to bed. Life didn't feel like living, I was existing. My core beliefs had risen once more: I'm not enough and I struggled to see a positive future.

When you feel like that, you find it so hard to see anything clearly and move on. I would find even with trivial things, such as watching the TV, I was triggered, often into panic attacks. My cushion became my comfort.

As I mentioned before, I always wanted to be independent. My relationship with my family wasn't strong, and so, I felt like I didn't have anyone to turn to.

However, I have a really close relationship with my daughters, which I am so grateful for. They have supported me through thick and thin, especially during lockdown when we'd video chat daily. Support and connections are needed to help each day bring some light. I felt really isolated and I think that's one of the biggest things that has come up: feelings of loneliness, even in a room full of people, no self-love or worth. I believed I didn't deserve to be happy.

I have since discovered that I have become really reflective as a counsellor and find it helps in my personal life too. I guess I've always been an insightful practitioner because I'm really reflective in my personal life, not just in my role. I do find this really hard, as it means looking back over things, to then help me understand and reach acceptance. There is always an answer, we're constantly digging for answers. I think that's what made it even worse: trying to find answers to problems. So, when I talk about problem solving, it's not like a right or wrong type of answer, it's more about knowing which tools to use, such as mindfulness, or going for a walk.

When my motivation is low, I find it really difficult to just go out for a walk, but then sometimes there's this little flicker of light in my head, which changes what I'm thinking and how I'm feeling, so I think, 'Right, let's go for it.' This is what helps me and I want to say as well that I'm really proud of my achievements. They're not always recognised within, like people who are close to me. But I'm very much at the stage now where I don't want to shout out loud and say, 'I'm a counsellor,' and 'I'm a children's creative counsellor.' So, I'm now at a stage where I'm developing myself still and I don't think you ever stop developing yourself. It's a massive thing.

Being in my fifties makes me think about things differently as well. It was around the time when the first lockdown restrictions were lifted, coming up to my fiftieth birthday, I realised it was time to step out of my comfort zone, which was a huge milestone. It felt like now or never. The following year I spent researching, completing trainings and workshops for preparation of starting my business.

In 2021, I was ready, and SR Counselling was born. I'd become a children's creative counsellor to support children and young people, ensuring they feel listened to and accepted for who they are. I feel it is important to offer intervention from a young age to help with worries, trauma, etc., instead of having no support until adulthood and experiencing an unhappy childhood like I did, which can cause mental health issues later on in life from keeping it suppressed for so long.

Over time, there have been lots of triggers from previous experiences that came up for me and I think one of the things I want to say is that during therapy I experienced a mix of emotions to allow healing to occur and get me to a place where therapy was no longer required, with an increased self-awareness to seek support when I can feel myself slipping.

I've created this bag of tools and resources, so I have ways to ensure self-care is in place. I've also realised, after years of wanting answers and a solution, that there isn't always one. I've learnt to love myself and say no when things don't feel right. I always go with my gut; I find it so powerful. I also find reflection helps me when I struggle. Using meditation and mindfulness with grounding reminds me I am not a frightened little girl anymore. I am an independent woman with so much to give.

I've found the more I dwell on the past, the more I think about it. I've changed my attitude and done a lot of forgiveness, so I can move on in my life with the people who are important to me. I'm now in a really good place. I love my job, I feel empowered, and my inner strength is stronger than ever.

So, I hope my story helps anyone who feels lost and hopeless. I was there once, but I'm here now and I want others to get here too.

I think one of the important things with this is to realise that even though I became a parent and started a family really young – I was just seventeen – it's never too late to start something new. There's always time and it doesn't matter how old you are. To know that you can get through these tough times and still be smiling, even if it's a small step, can count. If it's a challenging time, just the smallest step can be something like, 'Right, I've got up and dressed.' It doesn't have to be big, you know, just getting up and getting dressed sometimes, or even just having a shower, the smallest things can also count.

I'm still a single woman, but I'm also a strong and empowered businesswoman.

And you know what, to say that feels really powerful. As I'm writing it, I'm smiling, as if to say, 'Wow, what a journey. What a journey I've been on.' And I know that there's still more to come. And do you know what? You never know, this might be just the first chapter of my own book.

★★★

During my journey, there has always been a special person in my life, who believes in me. My Grandma Jessie. Certain reminders, even after she died, helped me continue when I felt like giving in. In one of those moments, I'd had a dream and she'd smiled at me; I was a little girl holding her hand. I felt warmth and loved.

Sam is the proud owner of the private practice SR Counselling, which opened in September 2021. She supports children and young people in a counselling role using a range of creativity and play.

Her background covers over twenty-five years in childcare settings. These include nurseries, children's centres, schools, children's residential homes, mentoring for The Children's Society, The Guide Association and recently a mental health support team. She progressed through her career and became a school counsellor, something she had worked towards since qualifying.

Sam qualified with a diploma in counselling in 2017, initially supporting adults, but after a short time realised her passion and belief was to support children. She then went on to complete a level four certificate with Place2Be whilst volunteering in several primary schools.

She is a mum of two daughters and a grandma of three grandchildren. In her spare time, Sam enjoys family time, walks in her local countryside, visits to the Yorkshire coast and the Lake District. Sam also practises mindfulness and grounding to relieve stress.

https://linktr.ee/sr_counselling

Listen to the audio version here:
https://bit.ly/MyJourneyofSelfDiscovery

HOW CAN SOMEONE ON THE INSIDE FEEL LIKE SUCH AN OUTSIDER?

Jen Rogers

The stadium buzzed with excitement. Yes, there was a football game our team was likely to win, but the game wasn't the buzzing highlight of the evening. This special night featured a nod to high school seniors and their parents before the ready-to-conquer-the-world young men demonstrated their prowess on either side of the fifty-yard line.

My stepson loves the limelight, and this would be his kind of night. The coach would be proclaiming his accomplishments and graduation plans over the stadium loudspeaker while he walked onto the field with his parents.

I know all about Senior Night. I'd been here years before with my two older daughters. I know this is an important milestone in a high school athlete's life. I also know the school administration plans this pivotal event months in advance. One key aspect of preparation would be the intake form given to the students to ask for information on their academic achievements, scholarships, post-graduation plans, and... the names of their parents.

My anger simmered as my thoughts lingered on how that intake form was likely completed. I know my stepson well enough to know my name would not be on it. At the time of his graduation, we had been a stepfamily for five tumultuous years.

Paradoxically, my husband Bill would have no idea of the school's preparation process. He often hovers at 30,000 feet, creating, envisioning, and imagining what's possible. I thrive on organisation and details when I'm not co-piloting with my man (or attempting to help him land the plane on the runway reserved for "superplanners").

I'm not often at a loss for words. Yet, I couldn't string my thoughts together in a way to share my fear of rejection with Bill as we drove to Senior Night. Although he felt the coldness oozing from the core of my being, he didn't understand what led me to building the wall of silence.

Can you relate? Are you caught up in the confusing role of stepmom? Perhaps you're fighting over different parenting styles, dealing with a difficult ex, feeling isolated, or experiencing anxiety and doubts about the best way to handle a new situation in your blend. You're not alone. All too often, stepmoms ask themselves, "How can someone on the inside feel like such an outsider?"

We arrived early and sat down on the hot, sun-soaked bleachers together. A warm night for a football game, yet a perfect evening for the senior girls wearing off-the-shoulder fancy dresses and gowns. Five years in and here I was, feeling like I didn't belong – again. Encounters with Bill's ex-wife still created difficulties in our marriage and our relationship with his two sons.

"First call for parents! It's time to line up!" blared the announcer.

"Well, that's easy," I thought to myself. "No call for stepparents means I'm staying right here on the bench."

A cop-out line of thinking that aligned with my desire to avoid the hurt I knew was coming.

> For our struggle is not against flesh and blood, but against the rulers, against the authorities, against the powers of this dark world and against the spiritual forces of evil in the heavenly realms.
>
> Ephesians 6:12

Bill expected to walk down to the field together, but I was stuck. Clinging to the metal bleacher, I wrestled between honouring my stepson and protecting myself from yet another wound of rejection.

In that moment, clinging meant preserving my dignity. Letting go represented obedience: loving my husband and my stepson more than my pride.

Standing up, Bill extended his hand to join him on the field. Anger flashed in my eyes as I looked up. My best bud met my spewing sparks with quizzical ignorance.

Dread and resentment filled me. Why wasn't my struggle obvious to my husband?

What would you do in this situation? How would you be feeling? How would you want your husband to support you? Use the space below to respond.

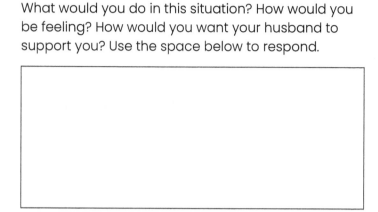

When couples decide to marry and create a stepfamily, the focus is rarely on the creation of a new blend. Their focus is on the joy and excitement of their love affair. And that makes a lot of sense in this starry-eyed phase of the relationship!

Love overlooks a multitude of faults... until those faults show up in custody battles, disrespectful behaviour from your kids, financial challenges related to child support or alimony, loss of intimacy as a couple, and the trauma of recovering from the hurt that precipitated the new family.

Despite the nuclear family no longer being the norm in many countries around the world, there are few resources available for equipping couples for the inherent and inevitable tumultuous blending. Marriage preparation courses do not address the distinct challenges stepfamilies encounter and many couples are unaware of the great help targeted, advance preparations offer. Couples can suffer tremendously under the stress of blending, leading many to divorce again.

What if there was a way to calm the chaos and prevent divorce?

Stepmomma, no matter where you are on your family journey, you are a woman of influence who can make a difference in your stepfamily life. Are there things you'll need to let go of? Yes. Will you gain more control when you give those things up? Not necessarily (in fact, you'll begin to see how little control you do have and learn how to be okay with less control). Can prayer make a difference in your marriage? Definitely. Will you experience more confidence when you identify boundaries that work well for you? Yes!

First things first. Let's start with you! The truth is, we simply don't have as much control as we would like to have. However, we do have influence. Our influence grows as our relationships develop in our blend.

Much of the confusion, rejection and isolation I experienced early on in my marriage was tied to unmet expectations. Sitting on that bleacher, I allowed past hurts to dictate what I was choosing in an effort to avoid future pain. I gave the fear of rejection power when I envisioned what it would be like to walk across that field and not be mentioned.

What past hurts do you have that may be influencing how your future will unfold?

Write a few of them down in the space below.

```




```

Back to the bleachers…

I had a choice to make. Participation or avoidance.

Reluctantly, I grabbed Bill's hand to head down to the field. I wanted to be joyful for my husband.

I failed miserably.

My husband's ex-wife waved us over. We found our spot near the end of the line, the privileges that accompany you when your last name starts with R. You know when you walk into a space and the air turns frigid quickly? Oh, the three of us were cordial and congratulatory, but the underlying barometric pressure indicated a storm brewing. We're like many stepfamilies who, when seeking adjectives to describe their co-parenting relationship, would say strained or difficult or complex.

I spied our graduate walking across the field at the same time I noticed oversized white buckets filled with long-stemmed red roses. I had forgotten about this Senior Night tradition. My heart rate elevated as I imagined nuking those roses with my eye lasers. I reminded myself to breathe naturally as I pushed away the image of rivers of red rose petals gushing out of the buckets.

I knew those roses weren't meant for women like me... they were meant for the "real" moms who would flash tear-glistened eyes like badges of honour. My eyes would remain dry, as if those buckets held only thorns of disappointment and accusations of, "You are less than. You don't belong here."

What girl grows up saying, "I want to be a stepmom"? Or "I want a bonus ex-wife"? I can name no one who would desire this awkwardness and discomfort. (I can, however, name many women who enjoy receiving roses!)

Are you harbouring anger or resentment towards your role as a stepmom? Ask God to strengthen you to better understand the stewardship role He has given you. Allow Him to work on your heart, so you can begin to release the emotions that create angst for you. Use the space below to write a note to God, asking Him to guide you.

Marginalisation cuts deeply.

Awkward moments happen regularly in blended families. As Bill's son made his way towards us in line, our eyes connected. I witnessed a slight hiccup in his step as he realised only one long-stemmed red rose would be plucked from the bucket for his mom.

There was a part of me who wanted to tell him, "I get it. No worries. We're all learning as we grow together." Another part wanted to scream and holler about all of the sacrifices I endured for him. How could he possibly forget about all I had done for him?

I clamped my mouth shut.

My heart grew harder.

We make jokes about the minds of teenage young men, but jokes are often based in truth – those guys do forget things! Their ability to see how their actions have an impact on others has many more years to mature. Does knowing that change the hurt? No, but it creates an opportunity for grace.

When have you felt marginalised or less than in your blend? What did you want to happen in that situation? How did you communicate your needs to your husband? Use the space on the next page for reflection.

The limelight moment...

As our son's name was announced, one excited senior and three co-parents began walking across the field. How many people scratched their heads when they heard two parents' names instead of three? I can only share that it felt like every eye was glued to us in that moment.

Walking in step with Bill and his ex, Bill and I on one side and his ex on the other, I was furious and deeply hurt that their names were announced together, as if they were still a married couple.

I felt shame.

This night was supposed to focus on celebrating our son's accomplishments and I was too caught up in my own pain to feel joy in my heart for this special event.

I felt embarrassed.

Anger simmered as thoughts rushed through my mind with each step we took. Was I really that unimportant in this family? Were we even a family?

I couldn't wait to get off that field.

And whenever you stand praying, forgive, if you have anything against anyone, so that your

Father also who is in heaven may forgive you
your trespasses.

Mark 11:25

For a while, I buried the hurt. Months would pass before I dug it up again, ruminated and relived it. Then, I let go of the hurt and, only through God's grace, I forgave my stepson. It took a little bit longer before I fully forgave my husband. Ultimately, I held Bill responsible for being unaware of the details of an event he'd never attended before. Forgiveness can be a hard lesson to practise when a woman's heart is hardened.

Are you harbouring resentment or hurt towards someone? Would you be willing to consider forgiveness at this time? Use the space below to record your thoughts.

What to do when you don't know what to do…
I had twenty-one years of marital experience before blending. Twenty-one years of pretending, wishing, failing,

desperate for a way out, dying a bit more inside each day in a marriage gone terribly wrong.

I was confident those difficult lessons learned in my first marriage would prevent so much unnecessary hurt when I remarried.

I couldn't have been more wrong.

At first, I figured I'd nail it as a stepmomma. I had decades of parenting under my belt, except I now had a bonus ex-wife, two boys who struggled with their new family structure and a husband caught in the middle of insiders and outsiders. Two years into experiencing massive rejection, frustratedly co-parenting an ugly custody battle, and the changing relationships I was having with my biological daughters, I was exhausted. I was tired of the other woman's disruptive influence in my home. I was beginning to hate everything about blending. My resentment and my feeling invisible increased simultaneously.

I had spent so much time dwelling on all the things I had lost after remarriage that I lost sight of the beautiful connection and intimacy Bill and I experienced when it was just the two of us.

I was fearful and ashamed that I might fail again, but stubborn enough to fight for what I knew could be. It was time to figure out how to make this stepmom gig stop feeling so impossible.

Even though I felt invisible, rejected, and very much an outsider, I knew those feelings weren't God's intention for me and my marriage. It was time to become an insider in my home. The result of this decision: two more hard years of missteps, misunderstanding, and missed opportunities as Bill and I searched for answers that didn't involve a divorce lawyer.

Then, we took all those mistakes and began to reframe them into our own kind of survival bootcamp, if you will. Instead of judging, we got curious about the triggers and learned from them. We established new ground rules and we worked as a team. We created a vision and a mission for our blend.

Soon, we'll celebrate eight years of marriage. Do we have it all figured out? Nope. We sure don't. But we *do* have the wisdom to be playful, intentional, curious and willing to learn. We've rejected the shame, pray together each morning as a couple, regularly practise forgiveness, and embrace God's best for our marriage.

There is hope in the hard of stepmomma life...

There is hope, Stepmomma, even when everything feels out of kilter. And let's face it, often things feel very much out of whack!

I want you to know you are not alone. Your hurts are real.

When we're the walking wounded, it's difficult to believe there is hope for our future. Yet, hope remains! Are you ready to embrace a change? Are you ready to focus on God's best for you and your marriage?

Let's gently lay aside the hurts and begin to envision the marriage and stepfamily legacy your heart desperately craves. Would you like to move from overwhelmed, anxious and exhausted to confident, calm and energised?

Look at the options below. Which will you choose to let go of? Which will you choose to embrace?

Overwhelmed Stepmomma	Action-Taking Stepmomma
angry	content
no desire for intimacy	intimacy is a priority
volatile relationships in home	peaceful home
on the brink of divorce	happily married
conflicting values	blended values
feeling lost	direction
feeling disconnected	family connection
hurting	healed
fearful	bold
doubtful and confused	confident
chaotic	calm
disastrous	exciting
alone/isolated	teamwork
uninspired	inspired
stuck in a rut	visionary

Which did you choose? How do you feel envisioning what could be? Use the space below to record your thoughts.

Next steps…

Find a stepmom community! We are created to do life together!

> Two are better than one, because they have a good return for their labour: If either of them falls down, one can help the other up.
>
> But pity anyone who falls and has no one to help them up.
>
> Eccelesiates 4:9-10

Without a community of people who empathise with our pain, isolation and alienation threatens our happiness. In a community of stepmoms seeking to build and live an adventurous, exciting legacy, you'll find the support and tools you need so you and your husband can truly blend beautifully together! If you'd like to join our virtual community, we'd be honoured to welcome you.

Relationships are desperately messy. And that's exactly why we need each other! It is within this mess that we are reminded of our need for Jesus, the ultimate healer. My prayer for you is that you feel loved, treasured and filled with hope! Blessings, friend!

★★★

To Stephen and Nathan, caught in the crossfire of the birth of one family mingled with the death of another, you are loved.

Are you ready to obliterate the notion that blending families is impossible?

Join Jen Rogers, a woman on a mission to make it possible for you!

Decades of life experience didn't prepare Jen for the challenges of combining families. Explosive communications, role confusion and desperation were the norm in the beginning. Now, with a growing understanding of what it means to work out your salvation with fear and trembling, Jen applies Scriptural principles for blended family victories.

Together with her husband Bill, Jen created Stepfamily
Mission POSSIBLE!™ Coaching Programs and
co-hosts their podcast, Stepfamily Mission POSSIBLE!™
that minister to stepfamily couples. Jen especially loves
coaching stepmoms!

Your mission, should you choose to accept it, is to learn
how to overcome stepfamily roadblocks and setbacks so
you can live your stepfamily legacy right now – without
all the stress and chaos. It's time to turn stepfamily chaos
into Stepfamily Mission POSSIBLE!™

https://linktube.com/missionpossible

Listen to the audio version here:
https://bit.ly/HowCanSomeoneontheInside

GIVING UP HOPE
IS A SUPERPOWER

Linda Barbour

"When we honestly ask ourselves which person in our lives means the most to us, we often find that it is those who, instead of giving advice, solutions, or cures, have chosen rather to share our pain and touch our wounds with a warm and tender hand."

– Henri Nouwen

"When you start seeing your worth, you will find it harder to stay around people who don't."

– Unknown

Just about everything you think you know about people and how they will behave towards you can be challenged by a toxic relationship, and even something as positive and life-enhancing as hope becomes a double-edged sword.

So, whilst I am writing a 'hopeful', 'happy ever after' kind of story about my own experiences, and those of the women I work with, one of the big lessons that I have learned is that relying too much on hope can get in the way of the reality of your life and making changes when you need to.

Without the belief that we can makes changes to ourselves and our lives, that good things and good experiences will come along, we can become anxious, feel powerless and get depressed, and eventually the 'hopeless' feeling will take over more and more areas of your life, but...

...*you can't live on hope alone.*

Hope can be a powerful energy to bring about change in your life or it can keep you stuck.

Waiting and 'hoping that things will turn out all right', can be a wise strategy, but it only works when you use it as an active choice, and not as a default, passive way of approaching life.

Using hope as a way of avoiding addressing problems, waiting for the difficulty to pass, or that something, or someone, will change to make the situation better can leave you as passenger in your life, and vulnerable to being exploited by other people.

When hope and optimism are combined with realism and trust in yourself, you feel confident, at peace and more in control of your life.

My Story

Like all of us, when we get married, I was full of hope.

For me, marriage was having someone by my side to love and be loved. Someone to care for and be supported by, a safe space where we could be honest and open and be ourselves. Build a life and family together. A partnership that was 'more than the sum of its parts'.

After fifteen years, on the outside, my life looked great. I was living the dream – married, living on a small farm, eating home produced food with two wonderful, healthy children. I was surrounded by beautiful countryside to ride through on my long-yearned-for horse, and doing a job I loved.

But on the inside, I felt deeply unhappy.

I tried to ignore it for a while, hoping that these inconvenient feelings would go away. I agreed with what other people were telling me. I had a good life with a good man – I should be more grateful and appreciative of what I had and not be so negative.

I was ashamed that I felt the way I did. Other people had much worse things going on in their lives.

Eventually, I was diagnosed with fibromyalgia – muscle pain, brain fog, exhaustion, depression, anxiety, problems sleeping – and I woke every morning wondering how I was going to get through the day.

It confirmed what I was told… that there was something wrong with me.

I was the problem that needed to be solved. If only I was all right, then everything else would be all right.

As a psychotherapist, I was used to looking within, and assumed that I would discover my issues, recover, and then life would be okay.

- Maybe it was the menopause, or that I needed to do more self-care?
- Maybe I needed to attend to my spirituality or financial well-being?

- Lose weight?
- Be fitter?
- Deal with my emotions?
- Change the way I thought?
- Spend more time with friends?
- Discover the generational cause?

I read loads of self-help books, did courses and worked with several gifted therapists and mentors and, to my surprise, everything I did led me to the same conclusion. It wasn't me that was the 'problem', but the relationship that I was in that was causing my difficulties.

Eventually I found 'The Covert Passive Aggressive Narcissist' (thank you from the bottom of my heart Debbie Mirza) – *'the most confusing and insidious type of narcissism'* – and the 'unreasonable behaviour' cited in my divorce started to make sense.

It is the mismatch between how he seemed to other people – a kind and caring man – with the way he treated me and the way I experienced him that led to my descent into a state of worthlessness.

I constantly doubted myself and I learned to ignore my feelings and instincts about things and, over time, believed him over myself. I saw myself through his eyes and saw how things seemed to him. I felt sorry for him to have to put up with me and my 'problems'.

Even now, writing this, I can imagine his responses to my experience:

- I always felt like he was going through the motions of empathising with my feelings, but it rarely felt real.
- It looked like he took care of me, but at the same time, what he did, and more importantly, didn't do, felt unhelpful and totally unsupportive to me.
- No matter how tired or ill I was, I felt bad for taking up his time, I felt how much he resented taking care of me.
- If I was hurt, or upset, I was too sensitive, had no sense of humour or didn't understand 'banter'. Sorry was not part of his vocabulary and any apology would be forced out of him.
- I was seen as someone negative, looking for problems and overly critical.
- I felt that things were always my fault, not surprising as I didn't do much right! My cooking was marked out of ten, and I never got a ten! (That was a 'joke' by the way, and, when I objected, I was told I had no sense of humour.)
- It wasn't until the children were old enough to say thank you to me for organising a good Christmas that I realised he never had appreciated any of the countless holidays and special occasions I had planned and executed. All I got was helpful hints about what I could do better next time.

And all that passive aggressive s★★t! So incredibly frustrating. Days where he wouldn't look at me or talk to me unless I spoke to him first and then he'd deny that was what he was doing. He'd ignore my feelings, 'forget' to do things, make little digs, be late, not say or do things that would be normal to expect (thank you, sorry, you look nice, for example), lots of little ways to provoke a reaction. How many times I got angry and shouted, looking like I was the bad, unreasonable one. It was easy to see myself as the problem.

> 'When someone is being covertly aggressive, they are using calculating, underhanded means to get what they want or manipulate the response of others while keeping their aggressive intentions under cover.'
>
> George Simon Jr PhD

All of this left me feeling like a crazy person… and worse, in a state of 'learned helplessness'. It seemed that nothing I did or said made any difference. It was Groundhog Day. Nothing changed, we had the same old endless arguments, with nothing getting resolved.

I was convinced that I was the one with the problem, the one who tried and failed to change my attitude, failed to be happy, or get anything right.

As I became more depressed, I withdrew from friendships and family life.

And the day I gave up hope that things were going to change, and I hit rock bottom, was also the day I made the decision to leave.

Looking at this in black and white with the benefit of hindsight, his unconscious manipulation and mind games seem obvious, but while I was in it, I couldn't see anything, except that I was ungrateful and inadequate as a wife and mother.

It was the loneliest time of my life.

Recovery

The divorce process is very triggering, and he became even more of a victim. I became very ill physically and mentally whilst he manipulated me and my solicitor wonderfully!

Recovery was slow. I stopped work as a therapist whilst I healed.

Like other women, it has been a struggle to explain to friends and family, let alone solicitors and other professionals what I have been through. Those who understand and have not judged me are few and far between.

I learned so much as I recovered and rebuilt my life.

I realised that I had become an over giver, a pleaser and developed poor personal boundaries. As an empath, I see the 'real' person underneath their vulnerabilities and insecurities and can be blind to the more obvious truths.

Traits that fed into the toxicity of our relationship.

I learned that living on hope alone, hoping that life will get better without any basis in the reality of your situation is soul destroying:

- Hoping that your intuition is wrong, ignoring its truth and not facing the reality of your situation only makes it impossible to keep trusting yourself and go to the loneliest place on earth when you disengage from your 'true' self.

- Hoping that you are the problem and so you can change the way you think, feel and behave so life can be better leads to constant feelings of shame, self-criticism and self-doubt.
- Hoping that being strong and resilient and 'if you just keep going' things will eventually get better means that we get physically and mentally ill.
- Hoping that giving someone else the benefit of the doubt and seeing the best in them will help them to change and be better people just leaves you vulnerable to being hurt over and over again.
- Hoping that, by sharing your vast reserves of caring energy, people will treat you in the same way that you treat them – with the kindness and respect you deserve – doesn't work and you give more and more, and inevitably get burnt out.

Giving up unrealistic hope has been my superpower. Accepting that people are not always 'like me'. By no longer projecting that energy on to other people and accepting good intentions as an excuse, hoping that they will change, I see other people much more clearly and will not get used or abused again.

So, hope now has to be firmly rooted in reality for me. In the words of my late Uncle William, "You can s★★t on me, but you can't rub it in."

So, I am not blinded by hope. I haven't lost my optimism and my absolute belief in the capacity of people to do amazingly wonderful, kind things for each other and for the world at large, but I do also know that some people will never change. They don't have the willingness or ability to. Now I judge people by what they do and not what they say. I see people more clearly and paradoxically am more accepting and less judgemental of other people and, most importantly, I trust my intuition when it says something is 'off'. Use your hopefulness wisely. Don't let it blind you to the truth.

★★★

To Debbie G.
For being there.

Linda Barbour is devoted to helping women recover from toxic relationships.

Because of her own experience of twenty-five years of marriage she knows that anyone, even the strongest, smartest, kindest women can have their physical and mental health destroyed by the people in their lives who are supposed to care for them most.

She uses her experience of recovery from complex-PTSD, rebuilding her confidence and self-esteem, and overcoming crippling self-doubt, anxiety and depression, along with her professional expertise to transform other people's lives.

She is a devoted mum to Marmite, her horse, and two decent grown-up human beings. If she's not at the stables, you'll find her renovating her home and garden.

https://linktr.ee/marmite01

Listen to the audio version here:
https://bit.ly/GivingupHopeisaSuperpower

BREAKING THE CHAIN, CHANGING MY FUTURE

Colleen Lee

"I won't let pain turn my heart into something ugly. I will show you that surviving can be beautiful."
— *Christy Ann Martine*

Hiding under my quilt, trying to drone out the sound of smashing glass and muffled shouting; one of my most revisited memories from my childhood. It was a regular occurrence back then. I take a deep breath and am grateful that my children will never have to live through the trauma that my siblings and I endured.

The youngest of three, I never thought that I would have been pretty much fending for myself from the age of eight. My sister, the oldest, seven years my senior, had faced the worst of my mother's wrath. Even when she wasn't drunk, it seemed that it was my sister that got the worst end. I think my mother found my sister's ways hard to deal with. Later in life, she was diagnosed with autism and taken into care at the age of fifteen. My brother was born with cerebral palsy, which affected his ability to walk, amongst other issues, although this never seemed to affect his sense of humour and his determination was commendable! He attended a residential school five days a week, only coming home at weekends. And then there was my dad: a hard worker who spent up to sixteen hours a day in work to provide for us. His gentle nature is an attribute I am glad to have inherited! Although, even the patience of a saint could have been tested by the fiery temper of my mam!

Despite everything, I could never hate my mother for her drinking. She was a strong, independent woman, stubborn to the core. Her childhood had been full of deprivation and violence. When her father died when she was fifteen, her mother had to take on two jobs, leaving the children to their own devices most of the time. My mother and her twin discovered alcohol. Married at eighteen and pregnant almost immediately afterwards, life was hard, but love kept her and my dad going. By the age of twenty-six, she had the three of us. My dad had to work, so she was our full-time carer, keeping the house going, back and forth to the hospital with my brother. He had countless operations to straighten his legs. I had cataracts, so also needed regular hospital visits, and it was at this point my sister went into care. As strong as she was, eventually the cracks began to show and I think the final straw was losing her brother to cancer.

She had begun to drink regularly. I always seemed to take it in my stride, though. When I look back, I don't feel sorry for myself, but the thought of my children in my position sends shivers down my spine. I quickly learned to fend for myself. Getting myself ready for school. Preparing meals for myself when she was too drunk to do so. I tried to help by hiding her drink when she'd passed out or giving it to my dad to dispose of when he got home This wasn't always the best option, though, as all hell would break loose when she awoke and couldn't find her booze! She had a heart of gold when sober, but the drink brought a very dark side out.

My dad did the very best he could for us, and we continued to survive. Then, when I was thirteen, I came home from school one afternoon and my mam had made tea for me, which I eagerly took and sat in front of the TV. When I'd finished, I went in search of my mam, only to discover she was gone! I waited until my dad got home and we went in search of her. After six weeks, we finally found out that she was staying with a man, also a drinker. From there on in my father filed for divorce and the choice of who got custody of my brother and I was put in my hands! It broke me to hurt my mother, but I knew my safest option was to stay with my dad.

For a year, life was quite stable, I felt safe. My dad met a lady and all seemed to be great, life was good! Unfortunately, it was not meant to be, because further down the road, after they married, I discovered she too had an addiction – she was completely reliant on Valium. This was okay, though, it didn't really affect me, until the GP decided to cut her off! She quickly changed, eventually turning to drink as well. Life was carnage for three years. She was violent towards me and would keep me home from school, threatening to commit suicide if I went. She was an epic liar and managed to convince my dad that I was just paranoid about alcohol because of my mam and a rebellious teenager who just wanted to split them up.

At the age of seventeen, I left home. I had recently begun to have contact with my mam again but couldn't stay with her because of her drinking. So, I stayed here and there at friends' houses until moving in with my boyfriend a few months later. My eighteenth birthday was a blast. My mam and her new boyfriend joined us for a few drinks, and I think it was the best time I spent with my mam since I was little, although I didn't appreciate how special it was at the time, nor did I know this was the very last time I would see her alive. Four days later, I got the news that she had passed away. She was just forty-four, the age I am due to turn on my next birthday. We eventually found out that it was an accidental overdose. She had taken her antidepressants and then gone out and got drunk. On returning home, she must have forgotten she had already taken them and took them again. My life became very dark. I'd lost the connection I'd had with my dad, my mam was gone and, by this point, my sister had moved to England. I felt so alone.

A few months later, I found out I was pregnant and began to set up a life with my boyfriend. Years passed and I loved being a mother, but it wasn't until I was in my thirties that I finally faced my demons. I had always just survived, suppressed my feelings and got on with things. But, looking back, I should have dealt with it all so many years earlier. Yes, I survived, and yes, I have been strong, but I know now that I shouldn't have had to have been. My relationship with my son's dad failed after thirteen years, and I have since married and had two daughters. I am proud of who I have become. I survived, and my children will never have to experience anything like I did because I will never allow it.

Back then, there was very little support, but today things are different. Never be ashamed to ask for help, be the one to help break the cycle.

I look back and I am proud, proud that I never gave in, proud that I can be someone my children look up to.

★★★

To my children, I hope I am the mother you deserve xx

Colleen Lee, forty-three-year-old mother of three (forty-three, when did that happen?!) married the love of her life and they are now living their best life. They say they aren't perfect and make mistakes, but learning from them and moving on is what continues to make them stronger.

https://linktr.ee/coll78

Listen to the audio version here:
https://bit.ly/BreakingtheChain

FROM FROZEN TO FEARLESS

Clare Ford

*"The day came when the risk to remain in a bud was
more painful than the risk it took to blossom."*
— *Anais Nin*

This is a story about rising up.

From Frozen to Fearless is the story of a woman who felt like she had lost everything, and that life was not worth living. This is the honest story of how she overcame depression, anxiety and grief in order to make difficult decisions with far-reaching consequences.

The important thing to understand is that this woman is just like you: an ordinary parent with an ordinary job. But now she lives an extraordinary and purposeful life full of passion and meaning because she is true to herself.

Have you ever turned up somewhere, looked about you and wondered how on earth you arrived there? Well, this is exactly what happened to me. One day, I "found" myself at the beach where I had gone for some important thinking time. A few days beforehand, I was actually considering taking an overdose, drifting off into a drug-induced sleep, free from pain. I had sat in my lounge, with sleeping tablets in my hand and antidepressants in my bloodstream, and actually considered how everybody's life would be better off without me in it. I felt at the time that I was a failure. A failure as a mother, a failure as a wife, a failure as a teacher… so who would really lament my passing anyway?

I couldn't believe that, at one point in my life, I had been traveling the world solo, trekking the Golan Heights, camping in the Sinai Desert, riding on camels, drumming in Martinique and so many more things I could no longer imagine doing. Now all I could think was how did I DO that? I can't even get out of bed to get dressed! On really bad days, I had to even ask a friend to walk my boys to school. I just couldn't face the chirpy "good mornings" and the pitying stares. I felt so disconnected from all the people around me. I felt completely adrift, swaying this way and that on the tide. I didn't recognise myself anymore. I couldn't equate the dynamic fun-loving person I had been with the shell of the person I had become, sitting forlorn and lonely on the beach… and part of me didn't even care. I had lost all sense of myself.

Have you ever felt like that? Have you wondered where the essence of "you" has gone?

Now, the reason that I say I had "found" myself on the beach is because, at that time, I didn't know what I was doing… I found that things happened without my knowledge! Somehow the chores were done – yet I wasn't really fully present for any of it. I was showing up but not connecting with my work, my family or my friends. I struggled to get up, to get dressed, to wash my hair. Even on better days, when people didn't know how low I was, I was really only playing a part.

I felt that there was no one I could turn to. No one I could talk to. You know that feeling of being surrounded by people but feeling so incredibly alone and isolated? I was tired of struggling and trying to please people being someone I wasn't. I tried to talk to people but I got the sense that nobody really "got" what I was trying to say. This created situations or problems when that hadn't been my intention. I felt like I was getting everything wrong. Eventually, I lost my voice and couldn't physically talk at all for what seemed like ages. Was this nature's way of telling me to stop banging my head against a brick wall?

Ultimately, it was up to me to fix this. So, I had to reach out. I put down the tablets and rang a friend, a nurse, who luckily had finished her shift. She knew of my situation and how difficult it was living in the same house as my husband while being separated. She knew about the work-related stress and depression. I told her about the tablets. I described how I longed for the peace and fuzziness to descend so that I wouldn't need to make any more difficult decisions. She told me that my boys loved me. She told me they needed me and that I could do it.

I listened and I allowed myself to be heard, helped and held.

That was all I needed at that moment and thank goodness I was given the opportunity to weigh things up for just a moment longer.

It is true that we are indeed creators of our own lives, but we are the destroyers as well.

That was when I had my light-bulb moment.

In that moment, I realised. I realised that I had to come back to me. I had to find my true essence. I had to reconnect with myself. I had to learn to love and forgive myself. No one else could do it but me. But I needed a bigger version of myself – something greater – a version where I could find strength and courage. I needed to feel connected internally to a greater source. I had to do it for me… to live!

I had to make a choice between life and death. And I'm not saying that to be overly dramatic or to elicit sympathy. It is simply what I realised in that moment… in that moment that proved to be the turning point in my life.

I understood that I could no longer play the part that I had been assigned. The words stuck in my throat and my feet could no longer traverse the well-worn stage. I was created for a different stage, with different actors and a different story. I had to change what I was doing, thinking and accepting. BUT I WAS TERRIFIED! Because I understood the emotional abuse. I understood my role and what I was expected to say, having practised people-pleasing since childhood. I understood narcissistic behaviour. I understood that I was a kind, loving and compassionate person who helped other people feel better. I understood that I had to protect my children from emotional bullying. I understood that I was playing the "middle class, living-in-the country, husband-in-the-city, teaching-in-a-village-school, belonging-to-the-tennis-club" game and I was good at it. Except it wasn't really who I was. The cap didn't fit.

With realisation comes fear. Because with realisation comes the need for action. For stepping out of comfort zones. For crossing new thresholds and opening new doors. And taking the dreaded "leap of faith". While I was sitting on the dunes looking out at the sea, I remember with absolute clarity imagining balancing precariously on a vertiginous clifftop. In my mind's eye, I was looking about me with a sensation of wonderment at the space... I had not felt so much space for a very long time... I filled my whole body with the blue sky. I breathed in it, and then, in my mind's eye, I prepared to jump. And that's when the voices started. "What if..." What if I don't make it? What if I fall and break something? What if I'm too weak? What if it's safer to stay where I am? What if I can't play the new role? If I fail the audition? What if I'm not strong enough? (I felt SO incredibly tired!)

NO! I knew that was no longer an option. I had to jump into the void. I had to take a leap of faith into an unknown future. I had to understand that I was being supported in my actions by a divine force. I HAD to say YES to myself. I had to learn from the lessons of the past otherwise I knew that they would keep repeating themselves – and had almost killed me. I couldn't take that risk again.

So, that's when I decided. I decided to leave my job. I decided to leave my husband. I decided to raise my boys on my own, on my terms, to model authentic relationships. I decided to get a better work-life balance. I decided to put my spiritual, emotional, mental and physical health first – for the first time in my adult life. I had no idea how I was going to manage any of this, but I knew I had to survive. I knew that I had a reason to be here – a calling, a mission – and that I was going to discover it. But I was SO SCARED! I kept having nightmares that I would be homeless, begging on the street with my boys, a bag lady. And I have been guided that this is actually what had happened to me in a past life… which is a story for another time!

After that, it felt like the world around me was amplified – the sky seemed bluer, the gulls louder, the sand whiter. I felt a rushing in my head and a lightness in my chest. I was under no illusion that the journey was going to be an easy one. But at least it was going to be one of truth. My truth. I also knew something else. That I couldn't make this journey on my own. That I was going to need help, and that I was going to have to ask for it. These were two quite new observations – ones which didn't feel very comfortable, if I'm honest.

My journey to wellness began with healing. I had heard of "healing" and had realised that antidepressants and sleeping tablets weren't healing me, rather numbing the pain (for which I was grateful at the time, I won't lie). I had even been told that I was a natural healer but ignored that for some years. Out of a mixture of curiosity and desperation, I located my nearest healer and paid what I considered then a lot of money for my first energy healing experience. Since then, I haven't looked back. The treatments were so effective. The easiest way to explain my transformation is to use the metaphor of a flame. When I first went for healing, I was broken, vulnerable, depressed and grieving. The flame in my belly was small and blue, barely burning at all. In fact, it had almost been extinguished. During a nurturing course of healing treatments, massages, acupuncture, reflexology, osteopathy, counselling and life-coaching, my flame grew brighter. I was adding the fuel I needed. I was adding compassion, forgiveness, kindness. I was adding self-care, self-nurture and self-love. I was taking my time.

I was also having fun. Some mums at the school gate possibly thought I went a bit crazy! I learned to fly a light aircraft – to see life from a different perspective. I started walking regularly, and then running. This reacquainted me with nature and again helped my perspective. I understood how I was connected with the rhythms of the universe. I understood how the seasons would come and go, whether I took action or not. Since that time, I walk every day and for me this connection with nature is crucial and beautiful. I reinvented myself. I had to get used to going out, socialising, meeting new people. I reignited my interest in music and live bands. I started drumming again. I started dancing again. I started doing activities that gave me joy and made me feel fulfilled. And I make a point of doing these activities regularly and consistently because I need them to be the whole me (not the flying, though – that was a one off!).

I also decided to contact my Reiki Master to train in Reiki healing myself. I set up my own practice and have helped women and children over the years with anxiety, panic, grief and stress, just as I was helped. Eventually, I decided the time was right to train as a Reiki Master so that I can attune my clients to help them with their own healing and that of their families.

Certifying as a life coach also turned my life around. I was able to leave my stressful job in teaching and set up my coaching practice, to have the flexibility I so craved. I am able to serve others, coaching and mentoring teens and supporting children with their personal development and spiritual and emotional growth.

During my recovery, I was prepared to do whatever it took to regain my health, vitality and zest for life, so I immersed myself in the study of meditation, mindfulness, NLP and healing modalities. Later, I became fascinated by modern neuroscience, the energy of the universe, the power of mindset and focus, and even quantum physics. I followed my gut instinct, and solutions and opportunities started to present themselves as I kept following my path. Because of this, I am able to use all the knowledge I have to help and serve others.

Of course, there are still bumps in the road, hiccups along the way, and a few mistakes, but it's all good. This is the beautiful journey of self-discovery, in all its imperfect glory.

I reach out for help when I need it. I know what I don't know (which is a LOT!) and I accept help and advice when it is offered with genuine intention. I choose not to dig so deep that I wear myself out. I am my business. My health and well-being are me. So, my health is my business.

I use my mentoring, teaching, coaching and healing skills that have been honed over the years to educate from a new paradigm, offering creative and intuitive routes that resonate with children and teens on a deeper level where they feel seen, heard and acknowledged for their strengths. I have been guided that this too is something that I have done in a past life as far back as the Saxon times. A teacher and a healer of women and children.

I am able to support my boys emotionally and practically and I am at home with them when they want me there. No guilt. NO GUILT! As a single mum – that takes some saying!

Our children are a reflection of us. How wonderful then that my seventeen-year-old son said he was glad that I divorced his dad. To say I was surprised is an understatement! But he went on to explain how we both seem happier. His dad has moved on and is in a healthy relationship with a lovely person. And I am too. But, more importantly, our boys can sense and see that. They can see that relationships can be different. They have understood that there is a way through. They know that to compromise oneself is not an option. My boys are supported and encouraged by me to step into who they really are and go for their dreams. And this is the greatest gift I think I can give my children. Alex is living out his dream and tapping into his passions as an artist and a filmmaker in one of the best art colleges in London, and Oskar is off to study history at university – like me, he has a passion for sixteenth-century historical fiction and drama. And they love seeing me living "on purpose" – stepping up to serve and make a positive difference every day with a smile on my face because I can and because I care.

Many people ask me whether I regret the things that happened to me, or if I would change anything. My circumstances, situations and crises have played a crucial role in creating the person that I am today. So, how I have chosen to perceive these experiences, and what I have chosen to learn from them, is entirely within my control. I chose to rebuild myself. I chose to plug the holes that were there from the heartaches. I chose to become whole so that I could unconditionally love myself before loving others. We cannot give to others what we don't have. In fact, that little sentence is so crucial that I am going to be indulgent and repeat it!

We cannot give to others what we don't have.

I have struggled with feeling different for so many years, feeling as though I was on the outside of everything, feeling trapped, suffocated, misaligned, and misunderstood. It was a really important part of my life journey to reach out for healing in order to become a healer myself. I could finally bloom! I came home to myself and to my reason for being here in this lifetime.

As it turned out, the universe had bigger plans for me once I actually stopped to listen, after years and years of hardship, and only when I was forced to listen against my better judgment. I finally listened to my heart and my intuition, and then my purpose finally revealed itself! It was like having permission to embody all my quirks, curiosities and magic and permission to understand life, people and emotions at the deepest level.

I could have allowed my lack of self-worth to continue to keep me trapped in a miserable existence; instead, I have chosen to turn my life around and inspire others, like you, to feel empowered.

So, spread your wings and fly.

I believe that every person is entitled to create a destiny that gives them the confidence to be themselves and to live a life with happiness, ease and abundance. To live with peace in their heart.

I live an authentic life – a life where I am ME, with all my glorious imperfections. A life where I embody my spirituality instead of hiding it; a full and abundant life… a life where I am an active participant, connecting with people from a place of unconditional love. A life where I can speak my truth and I am heard, acknowledged and appreciated. Simply for being ME!

Leading a fearless life.

***

I dedicate this to my two sons, Alex and Oskar.

Clare is an award-winning international author, speaker, coach, healer, educator and parent who is passionate about ensuring that children and teens are "switched on" learners, accessing their natural gifts, abilities and talents to discover their true potential and live purposefully.

Founder of SwitchedON!, the global online academy and an academic coach with over twenty years' experience, Clare combines her unique skill set using her SWITCHED ON! Learning Method to unlock the brilliance in your child, tween or teen.

Please connect with me further here: linktr.ee/ switchedonacademy1

Listen to the audio version here: https://bit.ly/FrozentoFearless

FINDING MY WINGS TO BE ABLE TO LEARN TO FLY FREELY

Emily Nuttall

*"Strength grows in the moments when you think you
can't go on, but you keep going anyway."*
– Conscious Magazine – Unknown

*"Be kind, have courage and always believe
in a little magic."*
– Cinderella

When we're born, we anticipate that life will be this
magical adventure of being in a fairy tale where you will
live carefree, safe, magical lives, healthy, loved, with no
worries in the world. But, sadly and truthfully, life isn't like
these fairy tales all the time like we would want, hope and
believe it to be. Life can be more like a storm of surviving,
rebuilding and growing through the unknowns, challenges,
hardships, pain and suffering to be able to experience the
sunshine and rainbows awaiting us on the other side.

So where does my story begin? I was born on the 4th
of September 1993. I was a premature baby, arriving eight
weeks early; I was very eager to come into this world,

weighing a small 4lb 4oz. After a period of time in an incubator in the special care baby unit, I was well enough to come home.

When your mother becomes pregnant, they go through a process of understanding the different development stages physically, intellectually, emotionally and socially, and are expected to meet key milestones at certain ages in all these areas. But I had other ideas and decided that detouring on meeting these milestones was much more fun and entertaining for my family; after all, life is about adventure, isn't it? After a range of tests, scans and surgeon assessments, I was diagnosed with cerebral palsy at one year old, which is a disability that affected my physical movement, development and some intellectual development, as a result of injury caused to my brain whilst my mother was pregnant. Adapting to the challenges and hurdles with cerebral palsy wasn't an easy ride, but with Mum, Dad and other family and professionals by my side, I knew I was going to be okay.

I recall one day at the age of three, I was sitting in the cottage drawing with my array of coloured pens around me. I drew me, Mummy and Daddy, all holding hands with smiling faces and all happy together. Little did I know that this would be the last picture I would draw of the three of us all together. Days later, after many months of Mum and Dad fighting, violence and arguing, Daddy walked out with no warning.

He chose a new life and family. My father figure I had bonded with so closely ripped my world apart.

A few months after my dad walked out, he had a new partner who became his wife six months later. It was decided that to help support my mum, I would spend half the week there and half the week at my mum's. For the many months and years that followed, my father's new home was a scary place. I had to regularly witness terrifying domestic violence between my father and stepmother, and I experienced emotional and physical abuse. My stepmother couldn't accept me for having a physical disability and for looking "different" to my siblings. She didn't want me to be a part of her "normal" family because I would ruin it, being a burden. Ingrained so deeply in my mind like a scar that never fades, she constantly screamed the words with physical actions that followed, including failure, useless, worthless, a mistake, fat, pathetic, disappointment and ugly. I was told I would never be loved. I would be excluded away from everyone and shut away in another room for most of the time I was there. It felt like I was locked in a prison cell, trapped, scared in the dark and all alone. This was a constant vicious circle of treatment I received. I believed every single word.

Being so young, I felt that I was a bad child because of what I put my family through with my physical disabilities and the many complex challenges that came alongside this. In my head, I interpreted that as needing to be and deserving to be punished. I was ashamed to be Emily. It led me to think why was I ever born? So many other children my age were so loved, carefree, safe, healthy and happy; what did I do wrong to not have this?

Aged four to eleven, I turned into a monster. Everyone thought I was just so horrible, bad and angry, but I was hurting and I had no way of expressing the terrifying fear, devastation and pain that I was going through. I buried it, internalised it in my head. If I told anyone, I would be the one to blame for ripping my whole family apart and ruining everyone's lives, or worse, I had the fear of not being believed.

Suffering in silence was so lonely and frightening I felt like I was trapped in my own bubble so desperate to be popped out of it but I didn't deserve anyone to care for or love me. So far, all I knew was hurt, fear, pain and suffering. In my little head, it made me question whether I was born to be punished, to ruin the lives of everyone around me.

I can always recall a question I was asked when I was in school of who my role models were, who I looked up to for guidance, protection, understanding, safety, love and support. There were three remarkable women: my gran, nan and auntie. Although no longer with me, they were like my guardian angels protecting me and keeping me safe. They recognised what was happening but they found it so hard to make it stop, as by this point the family courts were involved, making all of the decisions about my care. I had lost control of everything. I didn't even feel like Emily anymore.

By the time I was aged eleven to eighteen, I was referred to many services, almost like playing my own game of pass the parcel. These included the family intervention services, strong family teams, social workers, autism services, Action for Children and the CAMHS mental health and eating disorders team. Anorexia and self-harm had also become my way of coping. To everyone around me, I was always trying to show a happy and smiling face on the outside, whilst in reality I was broken, I was hurting, listening to my anorexia and self-harm voices, restricting my food and excessively exercising. Punishing my body is all I could concentrate and think about in my foggy, clouded mind. The physical pain it would give me every time I did not allow myself food and hurting myself would numb my emotions and give me that respite I desperately needed. I was angry and broken, but instead of directing that anger and brokenness at others, I directed it at myself because I never wished anyone, not even my worst enemies, to go through such devastation, pain, fear and despair.

I had described anorexia and self-harm to my treatment teams, friends and family as the best friend that I never had. Anorexia had been the thing I could run to when I couldn't express my pain, fear and despair to those around me or the terrifying things that were happening in my life. With the abuse, violence and family breakdowns, anorexia was my comfort blanket. I couldn't show anger because being angry was bad, as I was told "you're a fighter, you're strong, so show it", so it scared me to show weakness, fear, pain and vulnerability. But with anorexia, I could protect myself from all of that as well as escape the pain and devastation. Anorexia was a way to disconnect from reality, it was a way to shut down, to not have to be present in my own overwhelming, scary life, or be present in my own body or mind that didn't feel like mine anymore. To me, it was a slow and painful death. The weaker I got through restriction, cutting, suffocation and strangulation, the more I shut down. All I wanted to do was die and I felt anorexia and self-harm would help me get that. The more I held anorexia and self-harm close, the safer I felt.

Communication in my life had only been through anger, punishment or outbursts. I would be screamed at, shouted at and punished, therefore it made me believe I had to be punished. As I earlier shared, I had to put on an "I'm fine" mask. Anorexia allowed me to do that, but still somehow be strong. Even though both my mind and body were at breaking point, anorexia meant I didn't have to be Emily anymore. Who wanted to be Emily anyway? As far as Emily was concerned, she wasn't loved, needed or wanted. People who did keep me safe and relationships I did rebuild really wanted me to believe I was loved, worthy and enough, but anorexia took that all away from me. It wanted to protect me from any further pain, despair or hurt. Anorexia and self-harm needed me to make everything right and perfect in my life, otherwise it wasn't good enough. It gave me a sense of belonging, an escape from pain, fear and hurt, blocked out distress, fear, trauma, flashbacks, health challenges, voices and devastating life events. It has guarded me from the pain, protected me from people's judgements, actions and hurt, given me control, completely numbed me and been a way to be able to disconnect and forget, but yet still be this strong, smiling, determined, thriving, giving, achieving Emily for everyone around me in my life.

It's all about finding the courage to be brave, be vulnerable. As part of going back to my younger self, I feel this is something that is so important when we're making sense of what we have been through, when navigating traumas we have experienced in our lives in order to understand, process and make sense, to forgive ourselves as part of inner child work and give compassion to ourselves as we look back on our experiences, build, grow and offer a message of hope.

A letter I am about to share is part of my story of when I was fourteen years old. I had recently left a children's ward where I was being treated for anorexia and self-harm as a way of coping with the secrets of the abuse, trauma and family breakdowns. I was hiding a lot of my struggle and my story was regularly hidden behind a mask of "I'm fine". I often keep journals to document my pain and struggles, trauma, abuse, anorexia, self-harm and shame from what I was experiencing, as I often felt too ashamed to tell anyone what was happening to me at this time in my life.

But now I feel I can look back at this letter and hold that fourteen-year-old Emily, to comfort her and not be angry at her anymore. If you have experienced something painful like abuse or trauma in your childhood, I really encourage you to write a letter to your younger self too. You don't have to necessarily share this with anyone, but this could be something that helps you to reflect on your struggles, the journey you have been through and know that in the darkness, despair and pain of it all, the light at the end of the tunnel will be somewhere in sight. It will be a hard battle but worth the fight.

Dear fourteen-year-old Emily,

Today is Wednesday 27th of August 2008. You should be out with your friends, enjoying your final week of the summer holidays before starting your third year of secondary school. You should be safe, carefree, healthy, happy and without any fear or worry in the world.

I'm sorry that this is not the reality of what you had wanted and hoped for. I know that right now you are hurting, exhausted, broken, weak, alone and scared.

The four walls of your bedroom have become your prison cell. I wish I could have taken hold of your hand and hugged you, to be able to reassure you that everything is going to be okay. I wish I could have taken away your hopelessness, pain and despair.

I'm so sorry I didn't have the strength and hope that you desperately needed and wanted to be able to see the way forward.

Today the children's mental health, eating disorder and community nurses came to do a home visit, after your recent admission to the children's unit for anorexia and self-harm. I know you were furious and angry at their arrival after your mum finally revealed secrets that you had kept between you two right up until now.

I can recall the months before the start of

the summer term, and prior to this day, the feeling that you had convinced your friends, family, the mental health and eating disorders team, your doctors, physiotherapists, surgeons and family intervention teams that you were simply "fine".

But yet, you were far from fine, you were angry, broken and lost. Instead of directing that anger at others, you directed it at yourself.

The relationship between you and your mum was completely broken. You couldn't and wouldn't dare tell anyone of the emotional abuse that you were going through at this point at your father's house by your stepmother – the times that she would scream at you and call you worthless, fat, a failure, a mistake and ugly.

You could never explain how or understand why she blamed you for ruining her family unit, telling you that you didn't deserve to be in this world or the terrifying violence you would have to witness and abuse you would suffer physically and emotionally every time you went to their house between her and your father, and your suffering as a result. You hated feeling different because of your disabilities and personality and you didn't know who you were anymore.

So instead, anorexia and self-harm became

your best friends. It felt amazing to celebrate the "victories" of starving, over-exercising, strangling, purging, cutting, suffocating and hurting yourself until exhaustion hit every bone in your body. Your head was blinded by the pain of not eating, struggling to breathe from self-harming. It meant the flashbacks, thoughts, voices, feelings and everything happening went away.

It meant that together, you and your best friends could finally escape reality. This brought you so much relief, comfort and peace. It felt good and it helped you to feel safe and give you back that sense of control that you desperately needed and wanted in your life.

It was like a big blanket that you could hide under and be taken to your best friends' world, where you could celebrate the "victories" every day. You celebrated feeling numb and fading away to become nothing. You felt you could be free of this turmoil for good. Every day you would just be hoping and praying that by nighttime the exhaustion and the pain of all the harm would have meant that you could have just shut your eyes, gone to sleep forever and never woken up. You wanted to be free like a butterfly and no longer in this world, as morbid as it sounds now. Fourteen-year-old Emily had never been more desperate to die. You wished you had never been born into this confusing, isolating and lonely world you found yourself in.

All you could think about and plan in your head every day was ending your life. It would be the end of this intense, emotional and physical pain and distress. It would finally be over. But every day you had to live and say through your fake smile that you were simply "fine". You smiled even though you were in deep emotional pain and distress, even though your mind, body and soul were completely broken.

Emily, this was you at fourteen years old – Wednesday 27th of August 2008. You were broken and had lost all hope of ever seeing the way through this turmoil, pain and despair. You had simply just given up and you had stopped caring, but you were just a frightened teenager, who felt they had nowhere to belong or turn to in this unknown world.

Without anyone being able to see or understand the confusion, pain and despair that you were going through, you felt you needed and deserved to be punished; you were ashamed to be you.

Today is Tuesday 14th of June 2022 – it is exactly thirteen years, nine months and eighteen days later that I am writing this letter. You are now twenty-eight years old. If I was to give a reflection of what life is like now, I would see you, Emily, as a woman who is still on this journey in life, even though you still at many times wear your mask of "I'm fine" to hide behind and protect yourself and others, and continue to find and work on your sense of belonging in society and help you to cope when things are hard. You continue to be strong and brave enough to remove your mask to reveal the very strong but at times very vulnerable and broken woman beneath who continues to fight on this road of recovery to one day fully break free of the grip of anorexia, self-harm and mental health and offer hope, strength and encouragement to be able to help others to do the same and ultimately change and save lives.

Emily, you fight your demons, you face your fears, and you are realising it is okay and is important to be your own best friend after so many years of fighting, and to be proud of who you are and that you just as much as everyone else shines your own beauty and personality in your own way, and that really is okay.

Emily, being human, it is natural and normal to cry and break and learn from mistakes, but never give up because I promise you that you are loved and wanted in this world. Please be proud of the Emily you are becoming.

Remember, Emily, you don't have to face this battle alone, there are so many people who love and care about you, I can promise you that. Even though you may struggle so much to see it at times, there will always be someone there to hold your hand for as long as it takes.

For five years now, I have experienced life on the outside of an eating disorders and mental health unit and that is an achievement. So, remember this every single day when you feel like giving up, or giving in, because you just as much as every other person in this world deserves to be free and well and have healthy physical and mental health.

The world is waiting for you, Emily, go and grab it with both hands. A final word from me now to you, fourteen-year-old Emily:

Don't be ashamed of who you were at fourteen years old. Stand tall and don't give up, even when you are struggling, scared, distressed and exhausted of living, because you are going to come out stronger and it's going to be okay. I promise you can and will beat this. Stay strong – you can fight this. All I can say is that I'm truly sorry. Emily, I hope you can forgive me. You can make the future what we both want it to be, where our hopes and dreams finally come true. You survive, I promise. Believe you can.

All my love,

Emily x

What I have learnt from these experiences is that being honest and open was the bravest and most courageous thing. I've also learnt to be creative, to express what I want to say and share through art, writing and music. Sometimes going through abuse and suffering from eating disorders can be very confusing, lonely and isolating, particularly if there are other communication or traumatic challenges, which can make expressing oneself harder. But by meeting the needs of that person and allowing them to express in a way that is safe and helpful for them, it starts those really important conversations, tell a story and ultimately save and change lives.

Talk to someone you trust. Don't blame yourself. Life and recovery is a roller coaster of a journey, full of ups, downs, twists and turns, loop the loops and backwards drops. Healing is never a straightforward path.

Resources and strategies of support that can help children, young people and families who are at risk of abuse, domestic violence and family breakdowns include resources, coping strategies, support groups and helplines through charities such as NSPCC, Action for Children, Self-injury Support and Beat, the UK eating disorders charity. For adult survivors of abuse there is also an organisation called NAPAC (national association for people abused in childhood).

www.nspcc.org.uk
www.childline.org.uk
www.actionforchildren.org.uk
www.selfinjurysupport.org.uk

www.beateatingdisorders.org.uk
www.napac.org.uk

Things that really help me include journaling, writing and singing songs, playing the piano, music and art, using online support groups and helplines. For me, this is like having my very own life toolbox that guides, encourages, supports, inspires me and gives me strength and hope when faced with so much darkness and pain. It's the light shining through the tunnel that is waiting for me on the other side.

Finally, be proud of who you are, know that you're not the bad things that happen to you, you can be anything you want to be. Just know that, no matter what, you are loved, you are worthy, you are enough and each and every one of us has something amazing to offer this world.

★★★

I dedicate this book to everyone who is on a brave journey of healing and finding themselves again through the pain and darkness. You are a warrior, be proud of who you are, as you are loved, worthy and enough and have something amazing and unique to offer this world. The light at the end of the tunnel is somewhere in sight; it will be a hard battle but worth the fight.

I would like to acknowledge Cassie Swift for being a truly wonderful, inspirational mentor and guide for helping me to complete my chapter. I couldn't have done this without your reassurance, understanding, guidance and support.

I would like to acknowledge my trauma, mental health, eating disorder teams, social workers, safe guarders, family support worker and intervention teams, public protection officers, friends, family, my inpatient, day patient, outpatient treatment teams, surgeons, doctors, physiotherapist, occupational therapists, Action for Children, Talk ED, Victim Support, Self-Injury Support, Samaritans, NAPAC, Papyrus prevention of young suicide and Beat,the UK eating disorders charity, who continue to always be there for me, guide me, support me, and have given me hope and strength in the darkness, protected me from harm, kept me safe, allowed my voice to be heard and never given up on me. You have all continued to save and change my life for the better and for that I will always be eternally grateful.

Emily Nuttall is a motivational disability, children, young people, families and homelessness campaigner and advisor with Action for Children. Emily is also an incredible mental health and eating disorder campaigner, champion and speaker, disability sports coach with Guernsey Mobility Let's Go, MOE foundation coach, an entrepreneur and inspirational co-author of the books *It's Ok to Not Be Ok*, *Inspirational Women of the World*, *Time to Talk Mental Health Poetry Book*, *The Children's Mental Health Wellbeing Handbook* and she is currently writing her own book. Emily is an active fundraiser, campaigner and media volunteer for Beat, the UK eating disorders charity, she is a Health Connections community connector, Mind media volunteer and Action for Children ambassador.

Emily is currently embarking on her counselling skills level two to become a future counsellor, building and developing her Motivate the Mind business and completing her sports coaching and disability studies.

She has a background of studies in health and social care and previous employment with children and young people through the Guernsey Youth Commission. Emily is a trained adult and youth mental health first aider and has completed domestic violence awareness training.

Emily was diagnosed with cerebral palsy at the age of one, lost the sight in her left eye at the age of eleven, was diagnosed with scoliosis at the age of sixteen and spondylolisthesis at the age of twenty-five and is an inspirational woman who has overcome adversity. From the age of twelve, Emily has struggled with anxiety, autism, depression, self-harm, suicide, and anorexia and is a domestic violence and emotional abuse survivor. She

has overcome homelessness and family breakdowns and is a previous young carer. Emily is all about empowering people and inspiring long-lasting change.

https://linktr.ee/emilyn93

Listen to the audio version here:
https://bit.ly/FindingMyWings

SOMEONE ELSE'S LIFE

Jo Picken

"I am Jo and I have learned resilience…"

"Resilience is accepting your new reality, even if it's less good than the one you had before. You can fight it, you can do nothing but scream about what you've lost, or you can accept that and try to put together something that's good."
– Elizabeth Edwards

This is a story about a girl whose life was swapped for someone else's at the age of seventeen, following a traumatic brain injury.

When you say to someone, "When I was seventeen, I had a traumatic brain injury," they immediately think you were in a car accident, had a fall from a height or hit your head on something hard. But no, that's not what happened to me.

Encephalitis took away my future, the future Jo, the unstoppable Jo who had the world at her feet. It changed everything – and I mean EVERYTHING. In a few short hours, everything stopped, and I was someone different. That virus has continued to change the course of my life ever since.

It's over twenty-five years since those events and I've only just started to reconnect with who I was and to tell my story. For years, I never said anything, I told no one, I never shared my story – no one knew, other than my close family. The few people I did tell looked at me in disbelief, often passing comment like, "You don't come across like someone with a brain injury." What the hell does that even mean?

Back then – pre-internet days – I never knew another person who had been diagnosed with encephalitis. I didn't have a community support group full of other survivors and felt incredibly lonely. The isolation from the world would continue for years, angrily trapped in someone else's life that wasn't mine.

So, what is encephalitis? According to the NHS website, encephalitis is an uncommon and serious condition where the brain becomes inflamed and swollen, as a result of a viral infection, a fungal infection or an immune system error where the body attacks itself. The usual triggers for it are the common cold virus, cold sores, chicken pox (main cause of infant encephalitis) and, more recently, according to the Encephalitis Society, it has become "associated with Covid-19."

Encephalitis is rare, only about 4000 people get it each year in the UK – that's about 0.6% of the population. Most of you will have heard the term meningitis, which is an infection of the cerebrospinal fluid (the fluid that surrounds the brain and spinal cord), but encephalitis goes far deeper than that. Often misdiagnosed, encephalitis is an infection or inflammation of the brain tissue itself, which forces the brain to swell within the skull, causing irreversible damage to the parts where the soft brain tissue presses against the hard bone. It is a serious, life-changing illness and can be life-threatening. Sadly, as encephalitis is often misdiagnosed as meningitis, the urgent treatment required is not always administered.

Encephalitis often starts as a virus with flu-like symptoms, but can rapidly escalate into severe headaches, stiff neck, aversion to light, confusion, disorientation, lack of coordination, seizures, loss of consciousness and sometimes death. Longer-term symptoms of encephalitis can see significant changes in people's personalities and normal behaviour patterns, and survivors of encephalitis are often left with speech complications, hearing impairment and/or sight difficulties. Also, a loss of limb control and poor fine motor skills are common too.

Some people get a diagnosis quickly, have the correct intervention and live a 'normal' life afterwards. Others, like me, are not so lucky and the impact of the virus is lifelong. Learning to live with the emotional, psychological and physical aftereffects can be tough. I was a lucky one, who didn't end up in a wheelchair (the words of a GP during my recovery). Sadly, 10% of all encephalitis cases result in death, which is about 400 people a year in the UK. All those years ago I had never heard of encephalitis. It wasn't something that most people knew about; even now most people have never heard of it before.

Up until catching a winter cold, I was just being Jo; independent, driven and with a passion for grunge rock music. I was a seventies baby, born in a seaside town in southeast England on a snowy day in April. Seventeen years later, with the world at my feet, everything changed in a heartbeat.

I had been an incredibly independent child, always off on an adventure of some kind, didn't need help with anything, didn't want help with anything. I always wanted to do everything and try everything, all at once, independently, on my own. I was at college. I hadn't enjoyed school, it was tough for me (since then I found out that I am dyslexic) and it never really made much sense. College, on the other hand, was a different story. When I joined the local technical college to do my A Levels, everything changed. I realised I COULD learn, I WASN'T stupid and was loving life studying media and film. I absolutely loved it, I was in my element, talking about films, TV and radio all day every day.

That Christmas was when my mum and dad finally gave in – after me talking non-stop about how amazing Glastonbury '94 was, they got me a ticket for the hottest show in town, Glastonbury's twenty-fifth anniversary. There were only a few months until the third weekend in June when I would finally be back in that field in Somerset, in front of the Pyramid Stage, watching my favourite bands play. I was living my best life. That was until mid-January 1995 when, three months before my eighteenth birthday, it all came to an abrupt stop.

It was the weekend and my friends and I had decided to go to see a late screening of *Pulp Fiction* at the cinema in our local town. We weren't quite eighteen, but we all got away with it. At the time, it was one of the most ground-breaking movies we'd ever seen. On the way home, we stopped at the fish and chip shop, got a bag of chips each and I promptly dropped mine on the road. I don't know what happened, they just fell out of my hand. It was the start of becoming unwell and the loss of my coordination. By Sunday teatime, I'd managed to cover myself in the liquid from a tin of tuna I was opening to make sandwiches. I didn't understand why it happened, but this was another indicator of me losing control of my hands.

I went to my friend's house that evening after tea to chill out and listen to some records. Her room was in the loft and there was a steep ladder going up to her room. As I was leaving, I slipped, bounced down the ladder and broke the banister at the bottom of it, bruising my back all the way up. I was in shock, I cried and didn't really know why I'd fallen. It was another warning sign of what was to come. I slowly walked home that evening feeling quite bruised and battered and went to bed. As normal, I got up the next day and went off to college, then progressively through the day I started to feel quite poorly as flu-like symptoms came on. I went downhill very rapidly. The college tutor found me curled up in the corner of the common room and called my parents to come and take me home. I went straight to bed and didn't eat.

During Tuesday, I got progressively worse. I had aches,

pains, shivers and a temperature, but most significantly I could not stand any light. I couldn't even take my head out from underneath the covers because the light hurt my head so much. Mum called the doctor who came out to see me on the Wednesday and immediately called an ambulance.

I was taken to the local hospital and that's where I stayed for two weeks. On arrival, I was put in a side room. I was too old to go to the children's ward and too young to be on the female adult ward. So, they put me in a side room on my own. All I remember was feeling so ill and being really scared; I didn't know what was happening.

Doctors came in and out of the room and I recall having a lumbar puncture, which took what seemed like forever as one doctor supervised a junior doctor taking his one – twenty-five-plus years later, my back is still sore. After forty-five minutes of trying to complete the lumbar puncture, they eventually managed to drain some fluid from my spinal cord. This procedure is done because spinal fluid can be an indicator of meningitis, which causes it to become cloudy. So, they drained some of mine to see if it was cloudy, but it wasn't and they didn't know what was wrong with me.

At that point, I'd perked up and started to feel better, which was due to the doctors draining some of the spinal fluid, taking the pressure off my brain as it had a bit more room. I felt a little bit better. I remember being offered food and having some beans on toast. My mum went home, it was nighttime, but not long after that I woke up and was sick. My buzzer didn't work, no one came, so I tried to go and find a nurse. I called out and still no one came.

Eventually, somebody saw the light flashing above the door to my room, told me off for being out of bed, changed the sheets and put me back into bed. After that, I don't remember anything, for months. Being sick that night was the last semi-clear memory I have until March 1995. There are flashes of images and lots of the events have been filled in by my mum, dad and brother, but I don't remember anything much at all. I don't know how I got home, I don't remember what happened in the intervening time or how I started to recover.

My mum kept a diary and noted everything that happened, which has kind of filled in the gaps for me, so I have lots of weird memories that aren't actually mine. They are real memories, but they are other people's. They are not my memories because I don't recall what actually happened, only what people have told me about the following three months of my journey.

What I do know is that I felt progressively worse and worse. In terms of being poorly, I shut down and withdrew from the world. I couldn't lift my head up. I didn't recognise anybody except for my mum. I didn't even recognise my own father when he came to visit me in hospital.

I felt I was just left in that side room, in bed with nobody to help. I couldn't do anything for myself. I could barely move, I couldn't wash myself, feed myself. I couldn't lift my head off the pillow even, it was incredibly difficult. My mum would come every day to care for me, wash me and feed me, as best she could. She would sit for hours stroking my head but apart from feeling her hand on my head, it's all a massive blank.

I had cannulas in my arms and in the backs of my hands with fluid going into them. I don't know whether I had any pain medication. I don't recall, but there was little intervention or help from anyone apart from my mother. We were just left to cope, and I still don't know why.

I've been told that people came to visit, friends and family. I have no recollection of people coming and I didn't recognise any of them, not even my dad, my brother, my grandparents, or best friends. I have cards and presents still in a box to remind me of that time, but I don't remember people coming in and giving them to me.

After two weeks in hospital, the doctors sent me home, even though there was still no diagnosis at that point. I don't remember going home or how I even got there. After the stay in hospital, life didn't return to normal. There were still a lot of blanks, but I started to recover with the help of my family. At first, I needed carrying everywhere because my coordination was so bad I couldn't walk, even to the bathroom. I needed help with getting up, getting dressed and getting washed. The lack of coordination affected my ability to feed myself. I lost a huge amount of weight, ending up less than seven stone because I couldn't feed myself and being fed and eating was just too tiring. Just using a knife and fork was impossible.

Day by day, I slowly started to improve, the physical improvements in lots of ways were easier. They took time but recovering from the psychological, cognitive and emotional effects took much longer; a lifetime.

As I recovered, it felt like taking baby steps every day. Like a toddler. "Today, Jo, we are learning to walk. We're learning to feed ourselves. We're learning how to get dressed, how to put clothes on in the right order." I was an adult, but I had to learn all over again all that I needed to do just to function as a normal grown-up person. How was an eighteen-year-old meant to learn to read and write again?

Yet, in amongst all those baby steps and the slow progress, was the absolute sheer determination to get back to me again. Determination not to give up and that I wasn't going to be told that I couldn't do this or couldn't do that because somewhere deep inside me there was that fiercely independent girl who wanted her life back. She didn't know how to get it back or what to do to get it back but her determination never waned.

Throughout this recovery period, I didn't receive any rehabilitation or intervention, recovery support, physical therapy or any other emotional therapy. The whole recovery was left to my family to oversee with my own determination.

In the spring of 1995, I finally got a diagnosis from the GP about what had been wrong with me while I was in hospital. I was finally told I'd had encephalitis and that I needed to take time to recover. My immediate response was, "Well, what about Glastonbury? I've got a ticket. And what about college?"

The GP firmly replied, "No, Jo, you won't be going to college for a while and I think we need to be thinking about not going to Glastonbury, as it's only two months away." The old Jo deep inside was so angry, angry at having the opportunity to go to Glastonbury Festival taken away, and she was not going to be told that she wasn't going. So, six months after a life-changing brain injury, she went.

I went to Glastonbury for the first time and had the best weekend of my life. Although, after my wedding day and the birth of my child, it is now ranked as the third best weekend in my life, but it will always be proof that I did it, I overcame tremendous adversity. In spite of how much memory I had lost due to the encephalitis, I have some vivid memories of that truly epic weekend.

It was after Glastonbury that it really started to sink in quite how much my life had changed, and I began to get stuck in a loop going round and round, turning everything that had happened over and over in my mind. Constantly ruminating and not moving forward, not recovering at the speed that I wanted to. Flashbacks of horrendous scenes that weren't even my life flashed before me.

I couldn't explain to people how it felt inside. I couldn't explain what it meant to feel like somebody had taken MY life and given me somebody else's instead.

I could no longer be that independent, loud and driven person I once was. I felt as if so much of my life had been taken away from me but I could never find the words to express what I meant. As I became more and more dependent on the people around me, the angrier it made me. I felt stuck. I felt trapped. I was forever wondering about the 'what ifs' and how my life would have been if I wasn't ill. Who I could have been and what life would have looked like.

I spent many years not having the words to explain how I felt. Never really understanding why I never felt like I'd ever grown up, perpetually stuck in the mindset of a teenager. Not really understanding the impact the brain injury had on me, and was still having on me. It's so much easier to explain physical limitations that I have been left with following my illness, such as chronic exhaustion, having a bulge on my optic nerve or that I'm supposed to wear hearing aids because I have significant hearing loss in both ears. Explaining to people that I still have general weakness in my whole body that has never returned to its full strength but much worse than all the physical symptoms is the feeling that somebody else has got my brain and my life. A strange feeling that my brain and my life were never given back to me in the way that they were before I was ill. That somehow my brain ended up being scrambled, like scrambled egg and then put back into my head so it was never, ever quite the way it was before I went into the hospital in January 1995.

Only now, over twenty-five years on from those events, am I starting to finally come to terms with my limitations and the gift that the illness gave me. Now I'm embracing the new meaning of who I am rather than running away from it. I am done with feeling ashamed and making excuses about my behaviour. I am done with feeling confused about why I behave and react in a certain way. I am done with masking who I am, just to fit in.

Maybe at times I wished I could have had a badge to wear to explain to people that I had a brain injury, so please go easy on me. Because I've never asked for dispensation. I've never asked for anyone to go easy on me. I never even told my previous employers. I've only ever needed people to be kind. I've tried so hard to work my way out of a really difficult situation that physically, emotionally, cognitively and psychologically limited me back to seventeen years old and I never caught up, forever stuck being somebody with a brain injury.

So where does that leave me now? Now I feel like I'm starting to embrace the person I have been since 1995 and starting to love the person I am today. If I can tell my story and empower someone to seek the help and support that they need then maybe I can stop somebody else going through what I went through. And maybe, just maybe, someone else will recognise their struggles in recovery from encephalitis or TBI and have hope that it does get better.

I know for a fact it gets better because, since that moment in time twenty-eight years ago, whilst I feel like I have lived someone else's life, I have achieved a lot. A hell of a lot. I eventually learnt to drive, I eventually gained a bachelor's degree, a postgraduate diploma, two teaching qualifications and had a career. I am now a qualified therapist and business coach. I'm married to my best friend and soulmate and I'm lucky enough to be the mum of the most amazing young man on the planet.

I've achieved so much in my life, and encephalitis has

taught me that I'm far stronger than I realise. Inside and out. Also, I learnt that if you put your mind to it, you can achieve whatever you dream of, no matter your starting position, no matter your limitations, no matter how insurmountable the dream seems. With determination, you can make your dreams happen.

★★★

This is my story – Jo's story – but it's also a shared story, shared with my mother, my father, my brother, my husband and son, who have all helped me build a good life. For that, I thank you.

Jo Picken is The Holistic Business Coach, teacher, trainer, mentor and confidence coach – she loves nothing more than to see people shine brightly and brimming with confidence. As of 2022, Jo is a master emotional freedom technique trainer of trainers (EFT/Tapping), neuro-linguistic programming (NLP) practitioner, Usui reiki

master and angelic reiki master/teacher. But, before this, she worked in education as a teacher for twenty years.

Her first experience of EFT and NLP happened when her life suddenly changed, and she struggled to overcome the issues this change had caused. To help herself recover, Jo delved deep into both modalities and went on to learn and qualify in the techniques that helped her on the road to emotional recovery.

Now her passion is supporting well-being practitioners and therapists (mainly mums) to develop their businesses' foundations, shine on social media and to grow in confidence to reach their goals!

Joanna Picken BA/BSC, PGDip, QTS, Cert ED

https://linktr.ee/Jopicken

Listen to the audio version here:
https://bit.ly/SomeoneElsesLife

PERFORMANCE ANXIETY AND BEYOND

Charlotte West

*"Never give up on your dreams, anything is possible, you
just have to believe!"*

– *Charlotte West*

I could say the title of this book is exactly what I didn't
have, or at least if I did have it, I had very little of it.

I grew up singing. All my life I've been singing, it's what
I wanted to do, I have done it from a very young age and I
don't know any different. I've had many singing teachers
along the way, who have given me different advice. I went
on to do GCSEs, A levels, an undergraduate degree and
postgraduate degrees. I already had performance anxiety to
a certain degree. I already got nervous when singing. It's
the fear of being vulnerable in front of someone, baring
your soul, being exposed and, with that, a fear of failure.

I was about fifteen or sixteen when I realised that I had
severe performance anxiety. I remember standing in front
of hundreds of people on a school trip to Edinburgh, where
I was asked to sing an Italian aria. Everyone was so excited,
but also nervous. I always got nervous when performing in

a new place and I thought it was normal. My anxiety was normal. My name was called, and I was asked to perform. I began to sing. Now I always got nervous. Being vulnerable in front of an audience can be terrifying. I began to sing, and within seconds, panic struck. I'd forgotten the words. I'd forgotten all the words except one phrase. I began to shake. My knees were trembling. My hands were sweating. I began to panic. I began to sing the same words over and over again. Don't get me wrong, the melody was absolutely vital, but as I kept repeating words, overwhelm hit me like a tonne of bricks. My hands were sweating. And I could feel myself slipping away. It was terrifying. As I got hotter and hotter, and more nervous, I began to feel dizzy. I began to sound like Mickey Mouse and then the world was dark.

This was just the start…

As my singing career progressed, and my singing journey started to take flight, I over practised, and didn't drink enough water. I spent long, late hours in the rehearsal room. I didn't warm up because my teacher told me it was not necessary. I had to be the best. I found my happy place and just kept going and going. I used that muscle over and over again. I tried to keep quiet on occasions, but university life doesn't allow you to do that because you're always out dancing, drinking and having fun with your friends. Until, one day, when I finished my degree, I was in a masterclass. I stood up, tried to sing and nothing! My performance anxiety tripled, my fear of failure went through the roof and I had no voice. I literally felt like someone was pushing down on my vocal folds. Every time I spoke it was so much effort I felt as if I was shouting all the time and only a very small whisper was coming out. I used to go out for drinks and signed to people using the Makaton that I had learned to advise them what drink I would like from the bar. It was utterly ridiculous, my voice was shattered.

I didn't warm up, I didn't sing. I hardly even spoke because I was too scared of damaging my voice. My parents have and always will believe in me, and they kept me driving forward. However, I needed reassurance from a professional that everything was going to be okay and that I was going to be able to sing. That I was going to have a career out of singing.

After months and months of not really knowing what was going on with my voice, and with a lack of understanding from the professionals, I went to see a singing coach at a very well-known, established music school, which I will not disclose. I wanted to know what was really going on with my voice. It was disheartening because I had no idea what was going on and how to fix it. I was beginning to become more and more distressed by the fact that I wasn't able to sing, which was the main purpose and is the main purpose of my life. On seeing this vocal coach, and having had a two-hour lesson, I was advised to not speak and not to sing for six months. This was like taking part of my soul away. I was distraught. The one thing I had worked on for so many years since the age of seven, I could not do.

I began to feel as if my identity as a singer had been taken away and was completely out of my control. With the best of my knowledge and guidance that I had been given, I didn't really speak and I did not sing for at least six months, possibly more.

To be honest, the thought of singing in front of others or even singing in my bedroom filled me with dread. I was extremely lucky to find a sympathetic singing coach who was able to build my confidence so that I could understand that I still had a voice that was in working order. It took months and months of determination, slow progress, worrying that my voice would disappear at any moment. My coach gave me extensive vocal warmups, strategies for performing and a sympathetic ear. I was so frightened of singing. With the support and love of my teacher and my family, I gradually got my voice back. Now, you probably think this is utterly crazy. I had my voice back and that's amazing. Now I could go and sing again. However, this is when reality hit home, that I couldn't just go out and sing again. Singing in front of your teacher and knowing that you have your voice back is one thing. If I made a mistake, it was in that one room where no one else could hear me. In the big wide world, that was a different league. The performance anxiety that was already there had got considerably worse because I didn't trust my voice and therefore, I didn't trust myself to produce a sound that I was happy with.

I was lucky enough to have some performance opportunities come my way. They were very low-key performances where I was in a safe environment and could perform freely. These were okay, but they were nowhere near the standard I expected from myself or where I had been previously. After years of training, I was so angry. I was disappointed in myself. Weeks and weeks went by of practice, trusting my voice and knowing that it was going to be okay. Every time I stepped out onto a stage or a platform, it just filled me with dread and, every time it happened, the sense of failure came rushing back, not only for myself but for those who had supported me, particularly my parents. I had failed.

I began dating a very talented pianist. My performance anxiety was slightly less when performing with another. It meant that the focus wasn't on me. I believed the focus was on the other person because, of course, that person was more talented than myself. We were offered the opportunity to perform in St Albans as part of the Paralympics in 2012. My voice was starting to get back on track. I wasn't just singing classical, I was singing for me. It was an amazing experience and something that I will honour for the rest of my life. I watched the torch pass hands in front of the community and, in my heart, I was so very grateful and couldn't believe my luck. To perform on the same stage as Tinie Tempah was brilliant.

As I stood at the side of the stage ready to go, I was absolutely petrified. My hands started to shake, my legs started to shake and my breathing went completely out of the window. I managed to breathe a little, but it was too high. It was not calm. I took a step on stage and there I was in front of hundreds of people instantly wishing for it to be over. But I knew that I couldn't let the pianist down. It was all in my head. I wanted to do it so much, I wanted to achieve that performance. My voice was very shaky. I couldn't move my legs. I looked down at the microphone, trying to calm my nerves. Don't get me wrong, this was an improvement. This was an improvement from passing out onstage in front of people. I had done it. I had performed on stage in front of hundreds of people. I was so proud of myself, but there was still doubt in my mind; a little niggle in my head had self-seeded that I wasn't good enough, I had failed my parents, I had failed my partner, that I just wasn't good enough to be a singer.

I was meant to be really proud of what I'd achieved. You don't get asked every day to perform at the Paralympics. Later that month, I also got the opportunity to perform at AIR Studios. My partner had organised for me to go along to a recording session with session singers. This is where professional singers are part of a recording, whether that be for TV, film, etc. I had the pleasure of meeting renowned directors and also had the opportunity to showcase my voice to them, which is practically unheard of. It was phenomenal. I got to speak to lots of other singers, musical directors, and lots of talented people. I thought that would give me the drive that I needed to start performing again. But no.

I still lacked self-belief. I tried to get one-off performances, wedding work, missed opportunities and took many different employments, many of which involved working with children. Most of the time, I avoided singing professionally, but still took lessons, taught a few students and would work towards my dream and then stop again! It was a vicious circle.

Years later, during lockdown, I finally decided that enough was enough. I had wasted so many years not believing in myself and not having the confidence to sing, despite teaching others. I had not long completed a postgraduate degree in vocal pedagogy, which is the science of the voice. How could I teach others to be confident in their singing, if I didn't have the confidence to sing myself? I'd spent thousands on singing lessons and heard so many times that I could sing as a professional. During lockdown, I was lucky to find a gentleman named David Juncos, who was delivering acceptance and commitment theory. This included a number of Zoom lessons that were to take place where he discussed my performance anxiety and did several techniques to relax my mind and encourage my confidence, including meditations. Every session, I got closer and closer to performing in front of him, in a safe space where I could express myself.

Everything was going really well. However, when the day finally came to perform over Zoom in front of David Juncos, I ducked out. I had done all of this work and I couldn't sing in front of him. Yes, there is no failure, only feedback. And I believe that every step that I have taken has got me closer to my dream. But I just couldn't do it. I was annoyed again with myself and found it incredibly frustrating that I could not sing in front of him. I continued the meditations in my own time and spent a lot of time thinking about how much I wanted to perform and give to others. Because, let's face it, when you are performing, you are baring your soul to the rest of the world. It is not just singing, it is not just performing like a monkey. When you go and meet friends or go and meet people for the first time and they say to you, "You're a singer? Can you sing now?" that always makes me laugh. It's almost like you're a monkey on stage and they expect you to perform.

Lockdown, as it was for us all, was a very interesting time. There were so many online courses. So many things to do to keep us all amused for self-development, and also for enjoyment. It worked in my favour massively. I was fortunate enough to do a photography course – which, by the way, is one of my other passions in life – where there was a day on impostor syndrome, and I met a lovely lady called JoJo Ellis. This was the start of a journey that I did not know would change my outlook on life and would also change my confidence and my outlook on my singing career. First of all, I did a course in impostor syndrome. And then I was lucky enough to do a five-day workshop. What I didn't know was that at the end of the course I was going to be gifted a prize as I had helped others along the way to increase their confidence and self-esteem. JoJo kindly gifted me a course that was going to transform my desire to sing. We spent weeks together, building on self-esteem, confidence techniques, journaling, mind mapping, meditations, group sessions and so much more. We could be mentored through things like impostor syndrome and all the things that we don't talk about in life. I had the confidence to face my fears. I was lucky to be offered some NLP (neuro linguistic programming) techniques that would work on my performance anxiety. Don't get me wrong, acceptance and commitment theory had pushed me in the right direction, but NLP literally changed my life in an instant and gave me the tools that I needed.

So, I had done all this personal development and discovered the wonderful world of NLP. My job at the time was working in an office and, during lockdown, I had the wonderful pleasure of working from home – or not, as some others may see it. I suddenly found myself committed to quitting my full-time job and within an instant that was decided. I left my full-time job as a revenues and benefits officer and decided that I would pursue my career in singing and as a vocal coach. Now, let's think about it. I had just got myself a mortgage to purchase my first ever flat and I had made the crazy decision to quit my full-time job, which, in themselves, are two of the most stressful things that you can do. With the help of friends and family, I managed to secure eleven interviews with different institutions, councils and private teaching, and just like that, in September 2021, I left my full-time job. I had moved into my new apartment and had no secure income. But, I secured six of the teaching positions and the world was right in front of me. Yes, the world was in front of me. And yes, I still had performance anxiety. It doesn't just go instantly with the understanding of NLP that I'd had. I spoke to my mentor JoJo and asked her if I could do the course in NLP to become a practitioner because it had helped me so much to overcome – sorry, not overcome, to assist with overcoming – performance anxiety. I decided that I would become an NLP practitioner. It had made such a difference to my journey, and I wanted to make that change in other people's lives. Also, I wanted to help other performers like me overcome performance anxiety and, if not overcome it, at least reduce it to a manageable level where they can follow their dreams.

So, that is where I am now. I am continuing my journey as a vocal coach. I have trained as an NLP practitioner, something that I thought I would never do. I am not saying that I am cured. I am not saying that I do not have performance anxiety. But it is dramatically reduced. And I am now pursuing my career in singing and following my dreams. I want to sing at the Royal Albert Hall again, to sing at weddings, the list is endless. I am living my dream.

I am incredibly lucky to now look back at my journey and see the young person that used to pass out on a regular basis. I see that the journey I've gone on and the vocal health issues I've had have led me to the position that I'm now in, including performance anxiety. It has given me the understanding and the knowledge to pursue a career as a vocal coach and allowed me to accept that I have performance anxiety but it is not part of me. It is an external part of me that I can manage and work through. It will be part of my journey and will always be part of my journey. That's something I will be grateful for and something that I will use in the future when educating others. It is my journey, and it is part of my development. It may be part of your journey too. And that's okay. It's okay for your journey to have its ups and downs and for you to look back and see how far you've come. It may have taken me longer than I would have liked, but I have gone from passing out at a venue to now continuing my journey as a singer.

We are all a work in progress. We are all here to make a difference.

★★★

For my wonderful mum and dad.
Without you, none of this would have been possible. Thank you
for all your love and support. You are my inspiration! Love you
xxx

Stylistically diverse, Charlotte's singing career has seen her perform as a soloist with the world-renowned BBC Philharmonic Orchestra at the Royal Albert Hall and, in 2012, at the Paralympic Games Torch Ceremony alongside Tinie Tempah, as well as a host of other venues and events.

Originally training as a classical singer, Charlotte graduated with a BA(Hons) in music performance in 2007. Following on from this, she gained an MA in community music in 2008.

After overcoming issues related to voice loss and performance anxiety, Charlotte found a desire to pass on the knowledge she had gained from her experiences. This led her to complete a post graduate certificate in professional voice practice, exploring the diversity of the voice, thereby giving her coaching the flexibility to meet the demands of her clients, children and adults alike.

Charlotte is always learning and considers herself to be a work in progress, along with her performance anxiety. With this, she decided to become a practitioner in neuro linguistic programming, which made a dramatic difference in her journey.

Charlotte's ethos is to empower young people and adults to have a voice that is heard, a voice that is nurtured, for people to love singing as much as she does and to have fun!

https://linktr.ee/charlottewest

Listen to the audio version here:
https://bit.ly/Performanceanxietyandbeyond

NOT AN OVERNIGHT SUCCESS!

Harry Mansfield

Your Hope Turned into Reality

Holding onto hope can be such a challenge when you are perhaps tired, or numerous things have gone against you, and you are continuously being tested. You could be in a time of your life where as soon as you get back up again you are, once again, knocked sideways by an event. When you know how to use your mind in the right way, it enables you to turn your hopes into reality, to achieve what could, on those bad days, seem impossible, and on those calmer days achieve so much more with huge success.

There are a vast number of things that you see other people achieve. Sporting events, tough charity fundraising efforts, military accomplishments, work promotions and so much more. What is stopping these achievements from being your achievements? The mental strength that is needed to achieve these amazing things is not there for only those people, it is also available for you to grab hold of so you can achieve your own goals and dreams; you just need MindPower Proficiency®. Take a moment to note down the things that you want to achieve because, with the right techniques, your mind will get you there. You will manage life's curveballs better and have greater successes. If you believe in something it can, quite literally, be really something.

The First Time!

I will never forget the first time I realised how powerful my mind was and I learned what I could achieve if I used it correctly. Like you, I have a list of things that I would love to do or want to achieve. For me, many years ago, I wanted to do a parachute jump and learn it well enough so that I could go on to skydive.

At the time, I was seeing someone in the military, so I was in the perfect environment to be encouraged and given the belief that I could and would achieve it. If I hadn't been surrounded by like-minded people, it would have been just me and only me and my mind to accomplish it. In reality, it is only ever us and our minds that get us to succeed and achieve. It could be pursuing happiness, completing a project, being successful at work, or learning a leisure pursuit; whatever it is, we can always achieve and succeed when we know how to use our mind proficiently.

Let's face it – why would you want to jump out of a perfectly serviceable aircraft at 2000ft?!

You Have It In You – I Had It In Me

I am massively fortunate to work as a mental strength consultant. Mental strength is the foundation of absolutely everything we do in life and is an essential skill to have. It is often life changing, and through having the knowledge of how to make your mind more powerful, your degree of success increases.

Whoever's mind I am training, we work towards Awareness of the mind, Challenging the mind and how to Transform the mind, so they can ACT in the most powerful and proficient way and, as such, I have become affectionately known as The MindPower Champion.

Due to Covid and lockdown, people are now thinking about their minds and mental health much more, but what is not yet recognised is that, like physical fitness and diet, to be successful, the right work has to be done throughout each and every day.

I have been a sports coach for twenty-five years, firstly as a riding coach and later as a rugby coach. Working in this field was the first time I got a real buzz from my work; seeing the improvement and the benefits that my clients got, not only from their chosen sport, but also from new skills, which translated into many other areas of their life; successes at work and in their personal lives.

Looking at both of these sports, when it goes wrong it hurts: a miss-tackle in rugby or falling off a horse. Challenges in life can also hurt and, whilst it is always fantastic to be supported by friends and family, it is, as I mentioned earlier, only us that can actually get ourselves "back on the horse" with success. You can do this too.

Childhood Challenges

I knew that I wasn't having a fantastic time whilst growing up. It isn't until you meet other people and their families that you learn that the way you have been living and what you have been experiencing might not have been right. I thought, because I knew no different, that what was happening to me was normal, even though I clearly didn't like it. I knew no different.

I was surrounded in my childhood by people who did not respect me, and I was being brought up to not question anything and do whatever was asked of me, even if it was abuse, in my case both sexual and emotional. Slowly, I shut down my mind instead of using it in a powerful and proficient way to attract the positives and manage the challenges that came from the abusive behaviour towards me.

I felt very unsafe, but I couldn't fight my corner to make it less uncomfortable and reduce the pain. My mind didn't allow me to be strong enough to put in a boundary that would relieve the anguish and distress. The abuse came from both home and school and, later in my adult life, when I had a more powerful mind, police cases followed to catch the perpetrators. At the time, because some of the abusers were family members, I did not have the essential support network around me. It was only me that was going to get myself through this, but I did not know how to use my mind to help me and so, instead, it worked against me.

Not being believed in, accused of lying and not listened to, and definitely not heard, was the daily pattern of life. Repetition is how we learn, and I was repeatedly using my mind in the wrong way and the abusers enforced that. I chose not to say anything or retaliate; what was the point? It would have only made things worse.

Inevitably, we are all a product of our experiences and for me it is no different. I had relationships with guys I should never have had because I had grown to learn that you did what the other person wanted, and as I had never had a say before, I did not know it was wrong and therefore didn't do anything to change it. The abuse made my mind and me continuously do and act the way other people wanted me to. It was repetitive, so my mind learned the wrong repetitive behaviour.

Mistakes from Childhood into Adulthood

Despite their behaviour towards me, I kept trying to keep in touch with family members. I thought I was doing the right thing, which was, of course, what was expected of me, and despite being an adult, I was not able to see what I was doing was actually reinforcing the bad.

I continued to have relationships where I didn't voice my opinion and just went along with what everyone else wanted. Friends commented that when they saw me with these family members and partners how much my personality changed; from being happy and bubbly to silent and walked over. Sadly, even my decision to marry was the wrong one and, whilst I will never regret it because I have two fantastic children, I have learned so much from it. Over time, my mental strength allowed me to confirm that leaving my husband was the right thing to do, despite the huge and ongoing repercussions.

However unpleasant, my experiences have made me who I am, and I am thankful for what I have learned. They have benefited my work dramatically and I am so happy to be able to pass these essential life skills on to my children.

We all deserve strong mental health, but people have not been taught how to achieve it, which is such a shame when it is such a powerful tool to have. Like anything in life, we have to learn how to do it. From when we are born, we learn to walk and talk, learn different subjects at school and college, any hobbies we want to do and the skills for our choice of work, and learning how to train your mind to be powerful and proficient is just another skill to learn. You can then turn your hopes and dreams into reality and allow yourself to live your best life.

Mental strength is often thought of as selfish because you have to prioritise yourself and, in my past, I certainly didn't and as such got walked over! If you don't put you and your mind first, you won't be the best version of yourself and no one else around you is going to get the best version of you, so everybody loses out.

My Passion Knocked Me Sideways

Whatever is happening in your life right now, you need something that gives you pleasure and makes you feel good. It doesn't matter at what level; whether you are looking to complete it or compete in it and looking to win. An interest outside of your personal and work lives is essential to improve how your mind works and for me it is eventing (competing in dressage, show jumping and cross country in one competition).

I began riding at the age of eight on a horse called George, who went nowhere fast! Despite the lack of speed, I had the biggest smile on my face and in my heart and eventing later became my passion.

The challenge of achieving this outside of work and family life with it taking up a great deal of time and money was hard. Firstly, the aim was to complete and then improve to be able to compete and, when I got there, the aim to succeed at a higher level. There is always a bit of luck that can help greatly, but, when the luck turns into large amounts of misfortune and your hopes and dreams are taken away from you, your mind is what enables you to manage the knock backs and keep moving forward towards your dreams.

My eventing, however well or badly I did, was a lifeline and to have bad luck take it away from me made everything else so much harder to contend with. In 2013, I finished a really successful eventing season and the plan for 2014 was to qualify my horse at the time for international competition. Early on in 2014, my horse became badly hurt with a tendon injury. The area of tendon was damaged so badly that there was more hole in that area than tendon. Veterinary science is amazing, however, and with the use of stem cells taken from my horse (and insurance to cover the cost!) the cells were injected into the hole, which allowed him to recover really well. Recovery was to be a period of two and a half years and with this news I felt broken. Within that time, there was to be no riding for many months, no time for him to be out of the stable and then, quite rightly, a very restricted and rigid programme to get him back up and running again.

With the unpredictability of a horse having been kept in a stable for many months, when I finally was back on board working through the training programme needed to strengthen his tendon, I was thrown off him and was, in turn, not able to ride for six months, putting back my eventing even further.

Both of us finally got going again and we were happily training once more to compete, aiming for international level, but after just a few months, once again, my horse had a tendon injury, this time in a different leg. Whilst the damage this time was not as bad, it would still take eighteen months for this injury to repair and the knock to me was huge. I had to dig deep and use my mind massively to get through this. Before having this horse, I had already had two competition horses sadly put down in one year. This bad luck really seemed never ending.

After the eighteen months it was me who then had

further accidents; I fractured my shoulder, which was two and a half years for full recovery and then the following year a fractured elbow – another six months off and a further year to get to full strength.

Me and my mind had been severely tested and my mind should have been completely frazzled! I am so thankful that I had the knowledge of how to stay mentally strong and was able to use techniques required to get me through the years of waiting and disappointment.

A Hit on the Head to Wake Me Up!

In February 2015, when my horse was in rehabilitation from his first tendon injury, I had a life-changing accident, a head injury, which was a hit on the head that woke me up! Prior to this accident, whilst I did know I had been abused, I did not realise to what extent.

Lying down in a dark room for six weeks after the accident, both necessary to recover and not able to do anything else anyway, my mind was all over the place and I did not really know what was going on. I remember after the accident I was trying really hard to walk in a straight line and failing miserably – I looked drunk! Sound and light were very difficult to cope with, watching television was definitely not possible, along with screens from phones, tablets or computers. I could only look at something if it was still! I even had to ask people that spoke to me to stand still or sit still because, if they moved, I moved involuntarily!

Over the weeks and months off, I saw that I'd had to analyse my mind to work out how I could move forward, both physically and mentally. From this, a huge change in me began to happen. Up until then, I had been living my life the way other people had wanted me to (except for a couple of things – my two sons and my eventing). I had allowed my mind to work subconsciously in the wrong way all my life, which, because of my abusive childhood, had stopped me from living happily and successfully.

To move forward, I had to go through the process of remembering the abuse that my mind had blocked out, use my mind to manage the painful feelings and emotions that came with it, and learn how to stop my mind from working subconsciously in a negative way. It wasn't until the accident that I realised my adult life choices were as a result of both the abuse and Harry's wall, which was very tall and very wide! Not having the benefits of mental strength had also resulted in numerous physical symptoms, which were stopping me from doing what I wanted to do, so much so that the medical team that had been looking after me had told me I would be living with these symptoms for the rest of my life. I do still have some head injury symptoms today, but I now know they are because of the accident and not from how I am living my life and the lack of mental strength.

My Mind

I needed to use my mind properly and effectively to not be consumed by my childhood adversity or allow the repercussions that led on from it into my adulthood to take over, as well as the disappointments of not being able to pursue my passion of eventing. Through using my mind the right way, I now have so much.

There are numerous scientific studies stating that the majority of our mind in day-to-day use is the subconscious part. This means we are using the part of our mind that is not fully aware and yet it influences our feelings and actions hugely. We are allowing this to happen and, if we don't train our minds correctly, we are living our life not at its best, either personally or at work.

I now use my mind correctly and am no longer the person who has little or no perception of what is happening in my life, but the person who knows what my mind is doing so I can make what happens in my personal life, my work life and my interests happy and successful.

Your Hopes and Achievements

Sometimes terrible things happen in life and some of you reading this will know that first hand. Sometimes it can be mundane and boring, but through training your mind, you learn how to turn hope into achievement with happiness and success.

Things that happen to you might or might not be your fault, but if you use your mind powerfully and proficiently, you can keep the good in and the bad out. Use it to see you – your talent, your intelligence. Your mind will stop you from throwing it all away and help you to believe and achieve.

Whatever your fears, your frustrations and the challenges you face, your mind will help you to dominate. See what is out there and embrace it. Hope, inspiration, happiness, dedication, courage and success; all created and achieved by you and your mind.

★★★

Dedicated to Bernie – my parachuting inspiration!

Harry Mansfield has become affectionately known as "The MindPower Champion" through her knowledge of how to use the mind effectively when hope is hard to hold onto.

She first realised how powerful the mind can be when training to parachute over thirty years ago. She has fused this knowledge together with her survival skills from adversity as a child, a life-changing head injury, knowledge from careers to date with proven scientific methods to create her registered behaviour model "The Transformation Triangle®"; how to be Aware of the mind, Challenge it and Transform it – ACT.

Having been a coach for over twenty-five years, with much natural talent, she is excellent at teaching how advantageous it is for any business, place of education or for someone to take the decision personally, to learn how the mind works and develop the skills for strength and success. Her training centre teaches MindPower Proficiency® and is a centre of influence training both online and in person to turn hopes of all shapes and sizes into realities.

https://linktr.ee/harrymansfield

Listen to the audio version here:
https://bit.ly/Notanovernightsuccess

OTHER COLLABORATIVE PROJECTS BY CASSIE SWIFT

Navigating Anxiety with Children & Teens shares advice, strategies and real life examples from a collaboration of 13 experts in their field. It focuses on ways to navigate different forms of anxiety, from how we frame the term 'anxiety', to dealing with terminal illness, to the very real mum guilt. The aim is to aid you in supporting our younger generation as well as reminding you that you are  not alone - there are many people available to help you on this journey.

The chapters share real life stories and activities on dealing with the many different forms of anxiety our young people face. With the added bonus of audio links, it also means it is accessible for everyone to benefit from. If you are struggling to navigate anxiety then this book is a must read for you.

Available now from Amazon: https://amzn.to/3P61Iwk

Lightning Source UK Ltd.
Milton Keynes UK
UKHW020814070922
408462UK00008B/996

9 781739 617912